Economic Values and the Natural World

15 95 a Malsh

Economic Values and the Natural World

David W. Pearce

The MIT Press
Cambridge, Massachusetts

First MIT Press edition, 1993

© 1993 David W. Pearce

This edition was published by arrangement with Earthscan Publications Limited, 120 Pentonville Road, London N1 9JN, England.

Printed and bound in Great Britain.

ISBN 0-262-16138-9 (hc)

ISBN 0-262-66084-9 (pbk)

Library of Congress Catalog Card Number 93-77257

Contents

List of illustrations

FIGURES

TABLES

BOXES

Preface

This brief volume carries forward the analysis and arguments that my colleagues and I presented in *Blueprint for a Green Economy, Blueprint 2, Valuing the Environment*, and, soon, *Blueprint 3*. Its subject is exclusively the way in which economists seek to 'measure preferences' for improvements in environmental quality and natural assets, or against their deterioration. 'Measuring preferences' is a clumsy phrase, but at least it tells us what economic valuation is. Phrases such as 'valuing the environment' (which I am as guilty of using as the next person) are really very misleading. Economists do not 'value the environment'. They observe that individuals have preferences for improvements in the environment and that those preferences are held with varying degrees of intensity. For over a hundred years there has been a highly developed science within economics for measuring this intensity of preference. Its practice is known as cost-benefit analysis (or, more logically in the USA as benefit-cost analysis, the hyphen also serving as a 'minus' sign). Perhaps because of the confusing terminology, many non-economists get rather upset at this idea of 'valuing' environmental assets in monetary terms. I hope this little book will help persuade them that nothing evil is afoot.

The departures in this volume include a more detailed explanation of why economists engage in preference measurement in the environmental context, how they do it, and how the results might be used. One of the ironies of the criticism of this approach is that the critics seem to have nothing to offer in its place, unless it is the random benevolence of political in-fighting or descriptive and generally unimaginative procedures such as 'environmental impact assessment'. Nor, to be blunt, have the world's environments fared very well under environmental policies which are almost entirely dominated by non-economic considerations of worth and value. Some ecologists espouse an 'energy theory of value' in which, instead of money, units of energy are used. But the problems of monetary valuation of preferences are as nothing compared to the misleading nature of energy theories of value, even though the idea of the fundamental nature of energetics in ecological systems is unchallengeable.

I have also tried to show the relevance of economic values to 'sustainable development' which most people regard as a 'good thing' even if they are not sure what it means or how to achieve it. Defining sustainable development does not seem to me to be very problematic. How to achieve it is far more interesting.

Once the idea of measuring preferences for environmental improvement is accepted, the next issue is how to do it. Rather than taking time out to show how economists elicit monetary values I have confined the technique to Appendix II. Even then, the discussion is brief because there are several good texts now on the procedures for monetary valuation (see the bibliography).

Appendix I is reserved for a survey of another issue that causes politicians and industrialists especially apparent concern: the role which environmental policy might have in slowing the rate of economic growth as conventionally measured (in terms of 'Gross National Product' – GNP). It is unquestionably true that environmental measures *can* impair economic growth. But there are several responses to that observation. First, nine times out of ten, it need not damage economic growth. So much depends on how the environmental policy is formulated. Using pollution taxes rather than 'command and control' techniques (such as technology-based standard setting) at least has the virtue of minimising the cost of the legislation, as a good deal of economics has now demonstrated. But pollution taxes also raise revenues, even though that is not their primary purpose. Those revenues can be 'recycled' back into the economy, displacing taxes on effort and enterprise such as income taxes and corporation taxes. The effect can be to enhance economic activity, not depress it. The truth is that scare stories about the costs of environmental policy are frequently a disguise for the fear of upsetting some special interest group. Governments that protest the effect of environmental policy on the level of employment are generally guilty of an appalling hypocrisy: after all, most of them have shown scant regard for the unemployed in their macroeconomic policies. Blaming environmental policy for its effects on employment, even if there was an effect, is hypocritical. Appendix I shows that, by and large, we cannot find much evidence to support the idea that environmental policy to date has had a negative impact of any significance on economic growth and employment.

Finally, I hope the case studies are useful in illustrating how economic valuation works and the kinds of results that have been obtained.

As always, I am grateful to Sue Pearce for her wisdom and patience in tolerating the time I spend glued to the computer screen and the histrionics when I (frequently) lose my source material; Daniel Pearce for embodying all the artistic values I never had; Corin Pearce for showing me how computers work; and Bluebody and Dillbody for being such objects of affection, even if fax receivers worldwide must be tired of receiving blank faxes sent by a Blue Burmese cat with a fascination for touch dialling. Special thanks are also due to Emily Fripp of CSERGE for the final editing.

DWP
London and Bedford, August 1992

Acknowledgements

An earlier version of this book was prepared as a background paper for the World Bank's *World Development Report 1992: Development and the Natural World*, World Bank, Washington DC. I am indebted to Andrew Steer, Dennis Anderson and the staff of WDR92 for very helpful comments on the previous drafts and to the World Bank for permission to use much of the material in that report. My debt to those whose work I have quoted and summarised will be obvious. The interpretation I have placed on those works is, however, my responsibility alone.

Chapter 1

The context of economic valuation

SCARCITY AND CHOICE

If the Earth's resources were available in infinite quantities, and if they could be deployed at zero cost, there would be no economic problem. Everyone could have everything they wanted without compromising each other's or later generations' wants and needs. It would not be necessary to *choose*. Choice becomes a necessity once it is recognised that resources are finite in terms of their absolute quantity, or in terms of the costs of extracting or using those resources. For example, oceans have a finite capacity to assimilate waste before the process of eutrophication sets in. Going beyond that capacity means that the further benefits of disposing of waste to the ocean have to be weighed against the costs associated with eutrophication - eg the loss of fish stocks. This kind of resource constraint is an instance of 'Malthusian' scarcity, after the Reverend Thomas Malthus. The limit can be exceeded, but only at a cost. The other main form of scarcity is 'Ricardian' scarcity - after David Ricardo. Absolute limits are not breached, but the cost of harvesting, extracting and using a resource rises. The global atmosphere might be an instance of a scarce resource in the Ricardian sense. As its capacity to receive and accommodate gaseous wastes from fossil fuel combustion, land conversion and chlorofluorocarbons (CFCs) is exceeded, so the surface temperature of the Earth may warm up with deleterious effects to human well-being. The 'price' of using the atmosphere as a waste sink is effectively rising through time as greater and greater demands are put on it.

Economist Kenneth Boulding characterised the contrasting views of the environment as a limitless resource with the modern view of its essential finitude as the difference between the 'cowboy' and 'spaceship' view of the Earth (see box). In the cowboy's vision there is always a frontier beyond which there is more space and more resources, all to

COWBOY AND SPACESHIP ECONOMIES

Economist Kenneth Boulding coined the phrases 'cowboy economy' and 'spaceship economy' to characterise the transition in human perception of the natural environment in the twentieth century. The cowboy symbolises man's view of the natural environment as a new domain, a frontier, to be conquered and civilised. The cowboy economy is an open system which is maintained by resource and energy inputs which then become wastes, or outputs of the system. This contrasts starkly with the economy as a closed system, in which inputs are, as far as possible, transformed into outputs which are then returned to the system through recycling and reuse. As mankind perceives the 'limits' of economic activity in terms of the effects on the environment, so economic activity should be reorganised to increase recycling and reuse of materials, and to substitute unlimited energy flows based on solar energy for the embodied solar energy of fossil fuels.

Boulding's vision has done much to influence the nature of environmental thinking. In its most provoking sense it can be taken to imply that the 'throughput' of the economy is not something to be maximised, but something to be minimised. What matters is not throughput (the economic analogue of which is GNP) but the *stock* of wealth, including the stock of knowledge and human well-being and the stock of environmental assets. The idea that it is this stock that needs to be maintained and expanded underlies a good part of the modern thinking about 'sustainable development'. The idea of concentrating on stocks rather than flows may, however, be justified for a rather different reason. It is not necessary to accept the view that stocks rather than flows determine well-being. The stock of wealth determines the *capability* to generate real income. If real income is what creates most human well-being – and in the poorer world it is difficult to see it otherwise – then increasing the capability to secure real income involves increasing the stock of wealth. This is consistent with the World Commission on Environment and Development's view of sustainable development.

Source: Boulding, K (1966) 'The Economics of the Coming Spaceship Earth', in H Jarrett (ed) *Environmental Quality in a Growing Economy* Johns Hopkins University Press, Baltimore

be conquered. In the spaceship view there is only a large but closed ecosystem fed by solar energy but with finite capacities to absorb the waste from the human economy. Environmental scarcity is therefore an ecological fact of life. Whether that scarcity means there are currently 'too many' people, or 'too much' economic output is, however, a separate issue. Finitude does not itself *necessarily* mean limiting numbers or activity if (a) our obligations to the future are not themselves of infinite duration, and (b) we can expand the benefits of 'growth' without deteriorating the environmental assets upon which we all ultimately depend. Humankind does know how to grow economically without degrading environments. The fact that it has managed to do that with only trivial success arises, in large part, from the fact that there is no level playing field between environment and economic development. Until the economic value of environmental quality is an everyday feature of the way we compute progress and, more importantly, the way we make economic decisions, then this imbalance will not be corrected and the environment will not be given a fair chance. That is why economic valuation is important.

As to population growth, it is very much harder to defend the view that we can afford to continue current rates of population change. In large part this has to be because either there is no real net benefit to families from large family size, or because population growth imposes other costs on the rest of society, not least through the degradation of environmental assets. Thus, while a finite planet will permit economic growth with environmental quality (if we are imaginative enough), it will not permit rapid population growth with environmental quality.

Given that resources are scarce in relation to human demands upon them, choices or 'trade-offs' have to be made. In the market place the individual has fairly clear information on which to base any choice. The product tends to be visible, its characteristics are generally well-known, and it has a market price. The individual's choice is then based on a weighing up of the quantity, quality and price on offer, subject to some uncertainty arising from incomplete information. But when *environmental* assets and services are involved there is often very limited information about the nature of the product in question, and, invariably, there is no price posted in the market place. Pursuing the global warming example, there is extensive uncertainty surrounding the likely impacts of global warming. Hence there is limited information about the nature of the environmental benefit from controlling global warming – the 'product' or 'good' in this case is the damage avoided by undertaking control measures. Moreover, the global atmosphere is not bought or sold in the market place. Its 'price' is not perceived. An additional complication is that many environmental goods do not act like goods in the market place: they are 'public' rather than 'private' goods. Public goods generally have the characteristics of joint consumption and non-exclusion. What this means is that when the good is consumed by one person it does not diminish the amount consumed by another person. A's consumption of clean air does not diminish B's consumption. Non-exclusion means that A could not prevent ('exclude') B from consuming the resource. This 'publicness' is one of the reasons why markets often do not develop naturally in environmental goods and services. Given that trade-offs have to be made, it is fundamentally important to know what is being traded-off against what. And we cannot know that unless we have some idea of the economic value of environmental assets.

CHOICE AND VALUE

Making choices in the context of environmental quality, therefore, is more complex than making choices in the context of purely private goods and services. What has to be compared is one priced good (the private good) and one unpriced one (the public good) – as when deciding to invest in air pollution control rather than new economic output capacity. Alternatively, the comparison may be between two or more unpriced public goods – air quality versus water quality, for example. To make comparisons involving unpriced goods, it is necessary to *impute a value* to the environmental good or service. The discipline of *environmental economics* has developed techniques whereby such values can be imputed (see Appendix II). In the market place individuals exercise choice by comparing their *willingness to pay* with the price of the product. They purchase the good when their willingness to pay equals or exceeds the price, and not otherwise. Imputing values involves finding some measure of willingness to pay for environmental quality. This is the essence of the process of economic valuation: it involves finding a willingness to pay measure in circumstances where markets fail to reveal that information.

This 'market failure' is important for the allocation of resources within an economy. If the production of specific crops involves using agricultural technologies which give rise to soil erosion, then the damage done by the soil erosion may well not be reflected in the choice of crop or technology. This may be so even where the costs are borne by the farmer growing the crops: future damage to crop productivity through soil erosion may be imperfectly reflected in choices made now. Market failure is more pronounced still when the costs are borne by agents other than the farmer – perhaps in siltation of rivers, ports and reservoirs for example. Failure to account for these *external costs* gives rise to a misallocation of resources in the economy, in this case through the choice of the wrong agricultural technology. Making choices better informed to avoid this misallocation of resources involves understanding the *value* of the external costs, and then finding a mechanism for integrating those values back into the original decision to choose a technology. Valuation may be imperfect but, invariably, some valuation is better than none.

PROJECTS, PROGRAMMES, POLICIES

The purpose of economic valuation is to reveal the true costs of using up scarce environmental resources. Choosing 'instruments' is the mechanism whereby the resulting values are reflected in decision-making. If the disposal of sewage to inland waters gives rise to loss of well-being then the value of that loss should be reflected in the private costs of disposing of the sewage. This might be achieved by taxing the sewage discharger, by setting some environmental standard for the effluent or the receiving waters, or by requiring the discharger to buy permits for the effluent. In general, the choice of instrument – tax, standard or permit – will not be affected by the value of the damage done, although the size of the tax, the allowable pollution with the permit or the standard will. The virtues of economic instruments – taxes, permits and other incentive systems based on altering market signals – remain even if valuation is not carried out. But valuation is essential if the *scale* of the tax or strength of the regulation is to be determined. In practice, valuation is the exception and not the rule, contrary to what some environmentalists seem to think.

Environmental standards are often set by criteria that incorporate some features of the valuation process. Health criteria, for example, determine many environmental standards in the developed world. Damage to human health would be an integral part of any valuation process – people will be willing to pay to avoid health risks from pollution and waste. But as there are often many other forms of damage besides health effects, using health criteria alone could impose its own distortions on resource allocation. A good deal of environmental policy is based on some idea of 'best available technology' whereby a regulator encourages the polluter to use the cleanest technology available, usually contingent upon some qualification about 'excessive cost'. In many other cases, environmental standards are set without any clear or detailed rationale. Many regulations, for example, are the outcome of responses to environmental scare stories and misinformed perceptions of hazard and risk. In such circumstances, economic valuation is helpful as a check on the criteria implicitly being used.

Valuation is relevant at all levels of public choice.

- In *project appraisal* the environmental impacts of any investment need to be estimated and compared to the other costs and benefits.
- In *programme appraisal* the value of environmental impacts similarly need to be integrated into the evaluation process;
- In *policy appraisal* environmental factors need to be treated on an equal footing with other costs and benefits so that sectoral priorities are not distorted. This is as important in choosing between marginal expenditures on, say, transport as against energy, as it is in choosing between conservation and development projects. Similarly, as discussed above, the setting of environmental standards should be informed by valuation analysis. In short, environmental valuation should be an integral part of:
  — sectoral priorities;
  — the balance between conservation and development; and
  — the choice of environmental standards.

WHOSE VALUES COUNT?

Economic values reflect individuals' willingness to pay either for benefits or to avoid costs. Typically, the values that count belong to those actually exercising the choice: the current generation. But it is a particular feature of environmental costs and benefits that they often accrue to people in generations yet to come. How are their values to be counted? This is the issue of *intergenerational incidence* of costs and benefits. Counting only the current generation's preferences biases the choice against future generations unless there is some built-in mechanism to ensure that current generations choose on behalf of future generations and take their interests into account. This potential bias arises because future generations are not present to have their votes counted. Whether they are present or not, future gains and losses tend to be played down in economic decision making because of the practice of *discounting the future* (see following box, and Chapter 3). Discounting is the procedure whereby gains and losses to society are valued less the more distant they are in the future, a procedure designed to reflect the

COUNTING ON FUTURE VALUES

Following the approach of the World Commission on Environment and Development (*Our Common Future*), sustainable development implies some general rule about not impairing the capability of future generations to achieve the same level of well-being as the current generation. But this is in fact a particular ethical rule for treating future generations. There are others. Choosing between rules is far from straightforward. Yet which rule is chosen will have potentially major resource allocation implications. Philosophers and economists have analysed the issues in detail. In broadest outline the alternative views might be summarised as follows.

Teleology

Teleology involves weighing up goods and bads and aims to *maximise* what is good. Goods and bads are broadly construed. Equality might be good, so that maximising equality would be a teleological approach. Maximising the economist's notion of 'utility' (preference satisfaction) would be a particular form of teleology – *utilitarianism*. The essence of teleology is that it permits a balancing of goods and bads or of one good against another – equality against utility, for example. The benefit-cost approach is teleological, being a form of utilitarianism based on preference satisfaction as a 'good thing'.

On the teleological approach it would be consistent to adopt a policy that made future generations *worse off* compared to present generations if the gains to the present are deemed to be greater than the costs to the future. Teleology is not therefore consistent with the broad definition of sustainable development entertained by the Brundtland Commission.

Theories of justice

There are several theories of justice. Some have been applied to the issue of how to account for the intergenerational distribution of goods and bads.

Contractualism
Contractualists argue that people will come together to determine rules of social behaviour because it is to their mutual advantage to do so. Laws and their implementation exist for this reason. This doctrine of mutual advantage will arise only in social contexts where the parties to the 'contract' are of roughly equal power. Otherwise the powerful would not secure any advantage from an agreement and they would not allow one to emerge. But future generations not yet born have no power at all, so the requirement of roughly equal power is not met. On the contractarian approach, then, there appears to be no basis for a theory of intergenerational justice. Even if there

were, it is inconsistent with teleology: justice would take precedence over the good.

Rights

On the rights approach, justice implies a duty to behave in a certain way, and confers a right on the person who is the subject of the duty to expect that behaviour. The rights approach is also inconsistent with teleology because what is right takes precedence over what is good. The rights are like constraints which must be met first before any other rule of behaviour is applied. The notion of 'maintaining wealth' (see the previous box) fits this approach since it is predicated on the view that future generations have a right to at least the same level of well-being as current generations. But there are problems of definition since it is not clear who holds the rights. Obeying the rule *now* would arguably alter the pattern of resource allocation which, in turn, would alter the behaviour of individuals even to the point of altering their decisions about family size or timing. The future population arising from the 'with rule' situation may differ from the population arising from the 'without rule' situation. There is no one in particular to whom the rights belong. This is the so-called 'non-identity problem'.

Resourcism

On this approach each generation should have the same level of resources or productive capacity as each other. Their well-being may then differ, depending on what each generation makes of this stock of resources. But their *capability* to generate well-being would be the same. Alternatively, since well-being depends on consumption and not productive capacity, what matters is productive capacity *less* savings.

Strict egalitarianism

Strict egalitarians insist on equality of some characteristic for each generation. It might be resource endowments (as with resourcism), or well-being itself. Or the rigidity may relate to the well-being of a target group, say the poorest group in society. No change would be permitted if the well-being of this poorest group was reduced, regardless of gains to other groups (John Rawls's 'difference principle'). Clearly, such approaches are inconsistent with the teleological view since none of them allows gains and losses to be weighed up independently of to whom they accrue.

Philosophical considerations may appear out of place in a discussion relating to world development, but it is fundamental to the way in which environmental issues are treated in economic appraisal. First, the conventional economic approach is based on a benefit-cost framework. Second, environmental problems often involve long-lasting or distant impacts. Applying the benefit-cost framework to environmental issues therefore poses a potential intergenerational impact problem. Resource allocation decisions will differ, perhaps markedly, according to the rule adopted for the treatment of future generations. The benefit-cost approach would permit gains and losses to be balanced between generations. Rules based on justice will produce different resource allocations since they invariably do not permit the trade-off between generations to take place.

Source: The definitions used here have been borrowed from Broome, J (1992) *Counting The Cost of Global Warming* White Horse Press, Cambridge

general observation that individuals simply prefer their benefits now and their costs later.

An analogous form of bias arises even within a generation: willingness to pay is weighted by the incomes of those expressing their willingness to pay. The economic votes of the poor count for less in the market place than the economic votes of the rich. This is the problem of *intragenerational incidence*. Because economic votes count more the higher the income of the individual expressing the vote, economic valuation appears to be distinctly 'unfair'. This is correct up to a point, and, for quite a long period in the development of economic appraisal techniques methodologies were developed for weighting the economic votes in such a way that this income bias was removed. Generally speaking they are not used now, although they could be. A practical reason why they are not used derives from the issue of what exactly one is trying to achieve by making such adjustments for varying incomes. If the aim is to reflect income distribution concerns in *all decisions*, then an income weighting procedure would appear to be sensible. But is it sensible to use income weighting in this way when society has other, more efficient, means to achieve distributional goals? For example, why build income weights into an analysis of, say, a tidal barrage if society can correct incomes for unfairness through the tax system? There do appear, then, to be some sensible practical reasons for not engaging in distributional weighting. Where those reasons are not persuasive, it is possible to introduce distributional weights (see box). Note that if we do not use distributional weights for *intragenerational* justice, we may have a problem in justifying a separate consideration of *intergenerational justice*. After all, the same problem arises. Why modify a project or policy to reflect intergenerational concerns when the current generation has a means of transferring wealth to future generations through savings and bequests. It seems fair to say that this is an unresolved issue within economics.

DISTRIBUTIONAL WEIGHTS IN COST-BENEFIT ANALYSIS

It is possible to 'adjust' cost-benefit analysis for distributional weights. Instead of adding up each individual's willingness to pay (WTP) one would add up instead:

$$(a_1 \times WTP_1) + (a_2 \times WTP_2) + (a_3 \times WTP_3) + \ldots + (a_n \times WTP_n)$$

for individuals 1, 2, 3 . . . n, where the 'a' is a weight. For example, if we want individual 1 to count twice as much as individual 2, set $a_1 = 1$, and $a_2 = 0.5$, and so on. Choosing the weights obviously introduces a further dimension into the cost-benefit study, but it has often been done. The weights often reflect some judgement about the 'utility' of an extra \$1 of income to one individual compared to another. In the example below, weightings of this kind were applied to the costs and benefits of a proposed new airport near London. The effect can be to alter the outcomes markedly compared to the 'unweighted' procedure.

The weight 'a' in the above formula can be obtained from the expression:

$$a_i = (Y/Y_i)e$$

where Y is the *average* income of the population affected by the policy or project, Y_i is the income of the ith person, and e is a measure of 'elasticity of marginal utility of income', ie the percentage change of an individual's well-being in response to a small change in their income. For example, suppose average incomes were \$1000 per month and the income of an affected group is \$2000 per month. The group in question is richer than average so we would expect the weight to be less than 1 if the weight attached to the average income is 1. From the formula, if the elasticity of the utility of income schedule is 2, then

$$a_i = (1000/2000)^2 = 1/4 = 0.25$$

so the gain to the richer group would be valued at one quarter the gains to the average income group. People with incomes below \$1000, say \$500 per month, would have a weight of 4 $((1000/500)^2)$, and so on.

Source: see Pearce, D W (1986) *Cost-Benefit Analysis* Macmillan, Basingstoke

Both inter- and intra-generational bias are therefore present in the willingness-to-pay criterion for eliciting economic values. They are deeply debated issues among economists. To recap, two reasons why they may not be quite as significant an issue are as follows.

1 Generations overlap: the current population includes three generations of parents, children and grandchildren. Parents care for their children and grandchildren and make sacrifices for them. Current children care for their children and will care for their grandchildren. In formal language, the rate at which current parents discount the future is likely to incorporate a 'coefficient of concern' for the future through the direct effects of children's well-being on parents' well-being. But how far care for the future is consistent with the kinds of discount rates used in *practice* (often 10 per cent in real terms, or more) is open to serious question.

2 Redesigning projects and programmes to allow for distributional fairness within a generation may be an inefficient way of serving the goal of fairness. It is often preferable to secure the gain to overall development by concentrating on efficiency gains and losses, and then correcting the distributional impacts in some other way (eg through lump sum transfers). Moreover, integrating distributional concerns into project and programme appraisal has been tried (Squire and van der Tak, 1975). It is not widely practised because of operational and informational difficulties. But care has to be taken not to use this argument to ignore distribution in the appraisal process altogether. More seriously, the same rationale for ignoring distributional considerations cannot be advanced so firmly in the context of *policy* choices.

There is no consensus on how to integrate inter- and intra-generational considerations into economic decision-making about the environment. While economists would typically favour the use of positive rates for discounting the future, some argue that there is no particular rationale for discounting future well-being. Most economists would probably focus on efficiency gains and losses in project and programme appraisal, but others favour the explicit recognition of multiple social goals or 'multi-criteria' and seek some form of calculus for trading-off between them when they conflict.

VALUATION AND THE DEVELOPING WORLD

Discussion of economic valuation and the role of future generations' preferences may seem remote from the concerns of the developing economies. But valuation is fundamental to the notion of *sustainable development*. If sustainable development is very loosely defined in the sense of the World Commission on Environment and Development (the Brundtland Commission, see World Commission on Environment and Development, 1987) as development that: '. . . meets the needs of the present without compromising the ability of future generations to meet their own needs', then it is clearly fundamental to know what is and what is not a sustainable development path. From the discussion so far, it should be possible to see that a development path which ignores the environmental consequences of economic change may well be unsustainable. As environments deteriorate, so human health will suffer from environmentally-induced diseases, and long-term labour productivity may decline. Degraded environments also impose costs in terms of forgone crop output due to soil erosion, additional energy imports as biomass energy is exhausted, diverted labour time to collect water and fuelwood from more and more distant sources, and so on. Moreover, when properly valued, investment in natural resource augmentation is often found to yield rates of economic return comparable to that earned on conventional capital investments.

Demonstrating that 'conservation pays' in economic development terms is a process that has really only just begun. But it is already possible to point to significant findings. Far from environmental and resource conservation being inimical to sustained economic development, it is in a great many cases integral to the development process. That is one of the messages of the remainder of this book.

Chapter 2

What is economic valuation?

It is important to understand what is being done when economic valuation is carried out. The economic value of something is measured by the summation of many individuals' willingness to pay for it. In turn, this willingness to pay (WTP) reflects individuals' *preferences* for the good in question. So, economic valuation in the environment context is about 'measuring the preferences' of people for an environmental good or against an environmental bad. Valuation is therefore *of* preferences held by *people*. The valuation process is *anthropomorphic*. The resulting valuations are in money terms because of the way in which preference revelation is sought – ie by asking what people are willing to pay, or by inferring their WTP through other means. Moreover, the use of money as the measuring rod permits the comparison that is required between 'environmental values' and 'development values'. The latter are expressed in money terms, either in a dollar amount or an economic rate of return. Using other units to measure environmental values would not permit the comparison with development values.

The language of economic valuation is often misleading. Studies speak of 'valuing the environment' or 'pricing the environment'. Similarly, changes in the environment affect health so it is necessary to find some valuations of changes in health status, the ultimate change, of course, being the cessation of life itself. It is commonplace to find references to 'the value of life'. Economists are apt to speak of 'the environment as commodity' which leaves them open – perhaps justifiably – to charges that this is all the environment is worth. All these terminologies generate an unfortunate image as to what the activity of economic valuation involves. What is being valued is not 'the environment' or 'life', but people's preferences for changes in the state of their environment, and their preferences for changes in the level of risk to their lives. There is no dispute that people have preferences for and against environmental change. There is no dispute that people are willing to pay to prevent or secure change: donations to conservation societies alone demonstrate this. The problem arises when this WTP is taken as 'the' value of the environmental change.

Many people believe that there are *intrinsic values* in environmental assets. They are of value in themselves and are not 'of' human beings, values that exist not just because individual human beings have preferences for them. There is no reason to reject the idea of intrinsic values because the idea of measuring preferences is adopted. What is being assessed are two different things: the value of preferences of people for or against environmental change (economic values) and the value that intrinsically resides 'in' environmental assets (intrinsic values). Economic valuation is essentially about discovering the *demand curve* for environmental goods and services: the values which human beings place on the environment. The use of money as the measuring rod is a convenience: it happens to be one of the limited number of ways in which people express preferences, ie through their willingness to pay. It risks the equation of money as measuring rod with money as Mammon, and since one 'cannot serve God and Mammon' the temptation is to think that one cannot serve money and the environment either. This kind of picture thinking is unfortunate, but understandable. Economists have been lax in thinking how their language is comprehended by others. And some non-economists have not, to be fair, made very great efforts to understand what economists do.

Once it is accepted that *both* forms of value exist, the issue becomes one of which values should inform and guide the process of making public choices. The answer is that since both values are 'legitimate', both are relevant to decision-making. Making decisions on the basis of economic values *alone* neither describes real world decision-making, nor would it be appropriate given that governments and the other agents involved in the development process have multiple goals. But one difference between the economic and intrinsic value approach is that economic values can, in principle, be measured. Intrinsic values cannot. If decision-makers do not feel the need for quantified assessments of gains and losses, then lack of quantification may not be an obstacle to decision-making. Otherwise it will often prove difficult to make choices between competing projects or alternative policies with differing environmental impacts.

The *practical* problem with economic valuation is one of deriving credible estimates of that value in contexts where there are either no apparent markets or very imperfect markets. If it is possible to derive such values, then it may well be that some measures of individuals' preferences will, in any event, capture at least part of what might be called intrinsic value. This will be so if the people expressing values for the environmental change in question themselves possess some concept of the intrinsic value of things. They may then be partly valuing 'on behalf' of the environment as an entity in itself.

Once again, the discussion may seem remote from the concerns of the development process. But it can be very important to those concerns. Many of the environmental assets that people generally feel are very important are in the developing world. Notable examples include the tropical rain forests, ecologically precious wetlands, and many of the world's endangered species. Many people feel these environmental assets have intrinsic value. They may express that view by speaking of the immorality of activities which degrade these resources, and of the 'rights' to existence of trees and animal species. Such discussions are important, but at the practical level the 'development and environment' debate is frequently about the very high value placed on development in a context of malnourishment and underemployment. The environment will often be viewed as a luxury to be afforded later, not now while the struggle for development is under way. Bringing discussion of rights and intrinsic values into the policy dialogue can be counterproductive in such contexts: honouring them is perceived as forgoing the benefits of development. If, on the other hand, conservation and the sustainable use of resources can be shown to be of *economic value*, then the dialogue of developer and conservationist may be viewed differently, not as one of necessary opposites, but of potential complements. The remaining stage rests on finding ways for the developing world to *capture* the conservation benefits. If environmentalists in rich countries perceive value in conserving a rain forest in a poor country, this is of little consequence to the poor country unless there is a potential cash flow or technology transfer to be obtained. Economic valuation is therefore a two-part process in which it is necessary to:

1 demonstrate and measure the economic value of environmental assets – what we will call the *demonstration process*; and
2 find ways to capture the value – the *appropriation process*.

TOTAL ECONOMIC VALUE

The economic value of environmental assets can be broken down into a set of component parts. This can be illustrated in the context of decisions about alternative land uses for a tropical forest. According to a benefit-cost rule, decisions to 'develop' a tropical forest would have to be justified by showing that the net benefits from development exceed the net benefits from 'conservation'. Development here is taken to mean some use of the forest that would be inconsistent with retention of the forest in at least approximately its natural state. Conservation could have two dimensions: preservation, which would be formally equivalent to outright non-use of the resource, and conservation which would involve limited uses of the forest consistent with retention of natural forest. The definitions are necessarily imprecise. Some people would argue, for example, that 'ecotourism' is not consistent with sustainable conservation, others that it may be. Accepting the lack of precise lines of differentiation, the benefit-cost rule would be to develop only if the development benefits minus the development costs are greater than the benefits of conservation minus the costs of conservation. Put another way, the development benefits minus both the development costs and the net conservation benefits must be positive.

Typically, development benefits and costs can be fairly readily calculated because there are attendant cash flows. Timber production, for example, tends to be for commercial markets and market prices are observable. Conservation benefits, on the other hand, are a mix of associated cash flows and 'non-market' benefits. This fact imparts two biases. The first is that the components with associated cash flows are made to appear more 'real' than those without such cash flows. There is 'misplaced concreteness': decisions are likely to be biased in favour of the development option because conservation benefits are not readily calculable. The second bias follows from the first. Unless incentives are devised whereby the non-market benefits are 'internalised' into the land use choice mechanism, conservation benefits will automatically be downgraded. Those who stand to gain from, say, timber extraction or agricultural clearance cannot consume the non-marketed benefits. This 'asymmetry of values' imparts a considerable bias in favour of the development option.

Conservation benefits are measured by the *total economic value* of the tropical forest. Total economic value (TEV) for a tropical forest is explained in the following box.

TEV comprises *use* and *non-use values*. Conservation is consistent with some sustainable uses of the forest, including sustainable timber harvesting. *Direct* use values are fairly straightforward in concept but are not necessarily easy to measure in economic terms. Thus the output of minor forest products (nuts, rattan, latex etc) should be measurable

TOTAL ECONOMIC VALUE IN THE TROPICAL FOREST CONTEXT

Total Economic Value =			
Use value		+	**Non-use value**
(1)	(2)	(3)	(4)
Direct value +	Indirect value +	Option value +	Existence value
Sustainable timber			
Non-timber products	Nutrient cycling	Future uses as per (1) + (2)	Forests as objects of intrinsic value, as a gift to others, as responsibility (stewardship)
Recreation	Watershed protection		
Medicine	Air pollution reduction		
Plant genetics	Micro-climate		Includes cultural and heritage values
Education			
Human habitat			

Total economic value comprises use and existence values. The use value category comprises direct uses (eg timber production), indirect uses (eg the protective effects of forests on watersheds), and 'option' values – akin to an insurance payment to reflect the value of a future use if the option to use the resource is exercised. Existence values comprise willingness to pay for an environmental asset's conservation even though no use value is present.

Economic values and tropical forest functions: the Korup National Park

Korup National Park lies in Southwest Province, Cameroun. It contains Africa's oldest rainforest, over 60 million years old, with high species endemism. There are over 1000 species of plants, and 1300 animal species including 119 mammals and 15 primates. Out of the total listed species, 60 occur nowhere else and 170 are currently listed as endangered. Continued land-use changes are putting substantial pressure on the rainforest. The Worldwide Fund for Nature (WWF) initiated a programme of conservation, centred on a management area of 126,000 hectares plus a surrounding buffer zone of 300,000 hectares. A similar programme was initiated for Oban National Park just across the border in Nigeria.

Economic valuation of the rainforest's benefits was carried out in order to assist with the process of raising development aid funds to conserve the area.

Benefits of conservation were then compared to the costs of the conservation project plus the forgone timber revenues. While the framework for analysis was the total economic value concept, existence and option values were not directly estimated. The procedure involved estimating direct and indirect use values *to the Cameroun* and then seeing what the existence and option value *would have to be* in order to justify the project. Since it was thought that the non-use values would mainly reside with people outside the Cameroun, the focus of attention for non-use values was on seeing what international transfers might be needed. Briefly summarised, the results were as shown below.

Benefits and costs to the Cameroun
(Present values, million CFA, 1989 prices)

(Discount rate = 8%)

Costs of conservation project:

Resource costs:	– 4475
Forgone forest benefits:	
timber	– 353
forest products	– 223
	– 5051

Benefits of conservation project:

Direct use benefits

Use of forest products	+ 354
Tourism	+ 680

Indirect use benefits

Protection of fisheries	+ 1770
Flood control	+ 265
Soil productivity	+ 130
	+ 3199

Net benefits to Cameroun	– 1852
Economic rate of return	6.2%
Net benefits to Cameroun if the discount rate is 6%	+ 319

From the standpoint of the Cameroun, the project appears not be worthwhile because there is a negative net present value of some CFA 1852 million at 8% discount rate, although there is a modest positive net present value if the discount rate is lowered to 6%. But the analysis covers only some of the components of total economic value. What of existence and option values? These were not estimated directly. Instead, the issue therefore becomes one of asking whether the rest of the world would be willing to pay CFA 1852 million (in present value terms) to the Cameroun to reflect these option and existence values. One way of testing this is to look at existing conservation transfers through debt-for-nature swaps. Translated into a per hectare basis, the required transfer for the Cameroun is just over 1000 ECU km². Debt-for-nature swaps have implied various valuations ranging from as low as 15 ECU km² (Bolivia) to around 1600 ECU km² (Costa Rica). Given the high species endemism and diversity of Korup, values of 1000 ECUs or more would seem justified. The conservation of Korup forest becomes justified in economic terms provided this transfer actually takes place.

The resource costs are based on budgets and plans in the Korup National Park Master Plan, net of compensation payments (which are internal transfers) and other costs regarded as being not attributable to the conservation project. The forgone forest benefits include timber from potential commercial logging (the 353 million CFA) and some forgone traditional uses of the forest, mainly hunting, that would be forbidden within a designated national park, and which cannot be offset by diverting activity elsewhere (the 223 million CFA). This proscription of traditional uses affects some 800 villagers within the national park boundaries. In the long run, however, other residents, mainly some 12,000 people on the periphery will be able to continue their traditional use of the forest, which they would not be able to do if deforestation continued. Thus, while one group loses, another, larger group gains (the 354 million CFA). The tourism figure is conjectural and is based on an eventual 1000 visitors pa by the year 2000 and their expected expenditure adjusted for the shadow wage rate.

The fisheries item is important. Rainfall in the forest feeds several rivers which feed into large mangrove areas rich in fish. The mangroves prosper on the basis of freshwater inundation in high water periods and saltwater in low water periods. If the forest was to disappear, peak flows from the forest would increase and there would be added sediment and less salinity. Basically, the mangrove swamps would no longer function as the habitat for the rich fish species that make up both the onshore and offshore fisheries. Since the link between the rainforest and the offshore fishery is less established than the link to the onshore fishery, only damage to the onshore fishery was estimated. This was valued at the market value of fish and, as a check, at the income derived from the fishery.

The flood alleviation benefits were calculated by looking at the expected value of the income losses that would accrue if there was a flood. The soil fertility benefits were based on a broad brush assessment that, if the forest disappeared, cash crop yields would decline by 10%.

The implicit minimum requirement for an international transfer (the so-called 'rainforest supply price') was estimated by taking the present value of net costs (the 1852 million CFA) and dividing by the present value of the hectarage that could be identified as being protected by the conservation project – some 500,000 'hectare years'. This produces the value of 3600 CFA per hectare per year, or some 1060 ECU/km².

Notable omissions from the study are twofold: no attempt was made to assess the value of the forest to local people over and above its use value; and no attempt was made to estimate the net contribution to CO_2 emissions from deforestation. Both omissions are likely to reduce the net present value deficit shown in the table. But only the former will lower the rainforest supply price because CO_2 benefits are likely to attract a negligible if not zero willingness to pay on the part of Cameroun citizens. The CO_2 benefits will, however, make it *more* likely that the rest of the world will pay for rainforest conservation (ie it affects the rainforest demand price).

Source: Ruitenbeek, J (1992) 'The Rainforest Supply Price: a Tool for Evaluating Rainforest Conservation Expenditures' *Ecological Economics*, vol 6, no 1, July, pp 57–78; Ruitenbeek, J (1990) 'Evaluating Economic Policies for Promoting Rainforest Conservation in Developing Countries' PhD thesis, London School of Economics; Ruitenbeek, J (1990) *Economic Analysis of Tropical Forest Conservation Initiatives: Examples from West Africa*, World Wide Fund for Nature, Godalming

from market and survey data, but the value of medicinal plants for the world at large is more difficult to measure.

Indirect use values correspond to the ecologist's concept of 'ecological functions'. A tropical forest might help protect watersheds, for example, so that removing forest cover may result in water pollution and siltation, depending on the alternative use to which the forest land is put. Similarly, tropical forests 'store' carbon dioxide. When they are burned for clearance, much of the stored CO_2 is released into the atmosphere, contributing to greenhouse gas atmospheric warming. Tropical forests also include many species which in turn may have ecological functions – one of values of biological diversity.

Option values relate to the amount that individuals would be willing to pay to conserve a tropical forest for future use. That is, no use is made of it now but use may be made of it in the future. Option value is thus like an insurance premium to ensure the supply of something the availability of which would otherwise be uncertain. While there can be no presumption that option value is positive it is likely to be so in the context where the resource is in demand for its environmental qualities and its supply is threatened by deforestation.

Existence value relates to valuations of the environmental asset unrelated to either current or optional use. Its intuitive basis is easy to understand because a great many people reveal their willingness to pay for the existence of environmental assets through wildlife and other environmental charities but without taking part in the direct use of the wildlife through recreation. To some extent, this willingness to pay may represent 'vicarious' consumption, ie consumption of wildlife videos and TV programmes, but studies suggest that this is a weak explanation for existence value. Empirical measures of existence value, obtained through questionnaire approaches (the contingent valuation method), suggest that existence value can be a substantial component of total economic value. This finding is even more pronounced where the asset is unique (see following box) suggesting high potential existence values for tropical forests and especially for luxuriant moist forests. Some analysts like to add *bequest* value as a separate category of economic value. Others regard it as part of existence value. In empirical terms it would be hard to differentiate them.

**VALUING PREFERENCES FOR UNIQUE ASSETS:
VISIBILITY AND THE GRAND CANYON**

Calculating existence value is likely to be important in contexts where (a) many people are familiar with the attributes of the asset to be valued, and (b) the asset is unique. Some evidence to support this view can be found in an analysis of valuations for improved visibility in the Grand Canyon region. By using surveys to assess both users' and non-users' willingness to pay (WTP) for improved visibility, one study found that user values were some 7 US cents per month, whilst existence values were $4.43 per month (1980 prices), over 60 times higher. Significantly, distance from the site did not affect preservation values, a fact that the researchers put down to the unique nature of the Grand Canyon, a 'wonder of the world'. Since distance was not relevant to the preservation bids, it is legitimate to extrapolate the mean preservation bids to the nation as a whole. The ratio of 60+ is much higher than other studies have found between total values and use values. But it arises partly from the uniqueness of the asset and partly because two different questions are being asked. The user value question asked how much users would be willing to pay *through entrance charge increases*, whereas the total value question related to monthly electricity bill increases.

Respondents were shown photographs of the Grand Canyon region with each photograph revealing different degrees of visibility. *Perceptions of* visibility could of course differ from some scientific measure, so tests were carried out which suggested a linear relationship between perceived visibility (on a scale of 1 to 10) and apparent target contrast measured by a multiwave telradiometer. Respondents were asked one of two questions: how much would they be willing to pay for improved visibility, with the 'vehicle' of payment being hypothetical additions to the existing entrance fee? and how much would they be willing to pay to preserve visibility if the vehicle was increases in the monthly electricity bill? The first group should therefore provide user values. The second group would provide a 'total preservation bid', ie user plus existence values. If existence values 'exist' then the latter valuations should be greater than the former. This was the finding. By showing how bids were related to income, age, and distance from the Grand Canyon, the WTP estimates could be extended to the nation as a whole and compared to the costs of controlling air pollution. The *annualised* preservation benefits for the nation as a whole came to $7.4 billion (1980 dollars) and the costs of control came to $2.8–3.1 billion in annualised form. Hence the costs of control were outweighed by the benefits of control by a factor of about 3.

Schulze, W et al (1983) 'The Economic Benefits of Preserving Visibility in the National Parklands' *Natural Resources Journal*, vol 23, January; and Brookshire, D, Schulze, W and Thayer, M (1985) 'Some Unusual Aspects of Valuing a Unique Natural Resource' Department of Economics, University of Wyoming, February (*mimeo*)

Total economic value can be expressed as:

TEV = Direct use value + Indirect use value + Option value
+ Existence value

While the components of TEV are additive, care has to be taken in practice not to add competing values. There are trade-offs between different types of use value and between direct and indirect use values. The value of timber from clear felling cannot be added to the value of minor forest products, but timber from selective cutting will generally be additive to forest products.

IS TOTAL ECONOMIC VALUE REALLY TOTAL?

It is tempting to think that economists have captured all there is to know about economic value in the concept of TEV. But have they? First, recall that they are not claiming to have captured all *values*, merely economic values. Second, it is not just environmentalists with their concerns for the 'rights' of Nature who feel uneasy about the economist's approach, but ecological scientists as well. Many ecologists share a philosophical or religious concern with 'stewardship' or a respect for the 'living' planet earth – Gaia. But many ecologists are also trying to say that total economic value is still not the whole *economic* story. There are some basic functions of ecological systems which underlie the ecological functions that we have been discussing (watershed protection etc). Turner and Jones (1991) call them 'primary values'. They are essentially the *system characteristics* upon which all ecological functions are contingent. There cannot be a watershed protection function but for the underlying value of the system as a whole. There is, in some sense, a 'glue' that holds everything together and that glue has economic value. If this is true, and it is difficult to pinpoint what is at issue here, then there is a total value to an ecosystem or ecological process which exceeds the sum of the values of the individual functions. Total economic value may not, after all, be total.

WHY DERIVE ECONOMIC VALUES?

There are at least five major reasons why economic valuation of environmental goods and services is important.

The environment in national development strategies

Environmental damage shows up in two ways as a cost to nations. First, it produces impacts on GNP: GNP is less than it otherwise would be if at least some environmental damage is avoided. Second, it generates costs which are not currently recorded as part of GNP, but which would be if GNP accounts were modified to reflect comprehensive measures of aggregate well-being rather than economic activity. Focusing on the first aspect, some evidence is now available to show that environmental degradation results in appreciable losses of GNP. The kinds of impacts that give rise to such costs include:

- forgone crop output due to soil erosion and air pollution;
- forgone forestry output due to air pollution damage, soil contamination and soil erosion;
- impairment of human health with consequent lost labour productivity; and
- diversion of resources from high productivity uses to uses such as maintenance of buildings damaged by pollution.

The empirical investigation of these losses at a national level is in its infancy. In the case of crop losses, for example, what is required is some measure of change in the overall level of economic surpluses (consumers' plus producers' surpluses are measures of the extent to which willingness to pay exceeds the actual amount paid) rather than a more straightforward estimate of crop loss valued at market prices. As an example of the former, the impact of global warming on world agriculture is under continuing investigation (see box).

VALUING THE EFFECTS OF DOUBLING CARBON DIOXIDE LEVELS ON WORLD AGRICULTURE

Economic models are being developed which attempt to measure the likely impacts of global warming on the world economy. One study shows the effects of doubling CO_2 concentrations on world agriculture, using a partial equilibrium world food model which measures changes in consumers' and producers' surpluses. Provisional results are shown below.

Table I *The effects of global warming on food consumers and producers*

Country/region	Welfare change ($m 1986)	As % of GDP
USA	+194	0.005
Canada	-167	0.047
EEC	-673	0.022
N Europe	-51	0.010
Japan	-1209	0.062
Australia	+66	0.038
China	+2882	0.141
USSR	+658	0.292
Brazil	-47	0.017
World total	+1509	0.010

Two results are of interest. First, the impacts are generally very small when expressed as a percentage of national income. Second, some areas gain from global warming due to the effects of the warmer climate on crop growth and suitability of land. The differences arise because of different climatic impacts in different regions: global warming will not result in the same temperature increases throughout the world. And precipitation will also change. The

notable gainers are China and the USSR. The overall impact on the world is very small at around 0.01% of world GDP.

Analyses of this kind assist in identifying the interests that each country would have in a global warming agreement. Those who gain are not likely to show much interest in signing an agreement, whereas those who lose might. On the other hand, the study assumes no 'discontinuity' in the relationship between warming and damage done. Sudden catastrophes and other ecological shocks and stresses are not allowed for. These might not be correlated with the 'losing' nations shown above, ie some of the expected gains may be offset by major weather events, while some of the losses might be even bigger.

Source: Resources and Technology Division, Economic Research Service, US Department of Agriculture (1990) *Climate Change: Economic Implications for World Agriculture*, Washington DC, November (draft)

Simpler approaches based on crop responses to soil erosion and pollution have their uses too. Soil erosion is endemic to many developing countries. Soil erodes 'naturally' but lack of investment in conservation, poor extension services, inability to raise credit and insecure land tenure all contribute to poor management of soils. A standard approach to estimating the costs of soil erosion is to estimate soil loss through the Universal Soil Loss Equation (USLE). The USLE estimates soil loss by relating it to rainfall erosivity, R; the 'erodibility' of soils, K ; the slope of land, SL; a 'crop factor', C, which measures the ratio of soil loss under a given crop to that from bare soil, and conservation practice, P, (so that 'no conservation' is measured as unity). The USLE is then:

$$\text{Soil Loss} = R \times K \times SL \times C \times P$$

The next step is to link soil loss to crop productivity. In a study of soil loss effects in southern Mali, researchers applied the following equation to estimate the impact.

$$\text{Yield} = C^{-bx}$$

where C is the yield on newly cleared and hence uneroded land, b is a coefficient varying with crop and slope and x is cumulative soil loss.

Finally, the resulting yield reductions need to be valued. A crude approach is simply to multiply the estimated crop loss by its market price if it is a cash crop. But the impact of yield changes on farm

THE COSTS OF SOIL EROSION IN MALI

The costs of soil erosion in Mali are shown using both the dose-response approach and the nutrient replacement approach. Because soil loss in any one year has effects in subsequent years, the data show both an annual loss and a present value loss expressed as a loss in a single year. Three conclusions emerge.

1 Economic losses from soil erosion are high enough to warrant conservation investments in some areas in the south of the country.
2 Investing in additional agricultural output may be less profitable than a simple financial appraisal would suggest. It is necessary to build into the analysis some estimate of expected soil erosion, and this will lower rates of return.
3 Most importantly, it is necessary to ask *why* soil erosion occurs. Restrictions on access to informal credit and insecure land tenure are important factors. High risks also contribute to high farmer discount rates: measures can be taken to reduce risks.

The nutrient replacement approach, which values the soil loss at the cost of replacing the nutrients, shows higher values than the crop-response estimate ($7.4 million pa compared to $4.6 million pa).

Table 2 *Farm income losses in Mali due to soil erosion (1988)*

(Loss based on USLE and farm budgets)	US$ million	As % GDP	As % agricultural GDP
National annual income losses	4.6	0.2	0.6
Discounted present value of income loss	31.0	1.5	4.0
National annual loss based on nutrient replacement	7.4	0.4	1.0

Source: Bishop, J and Allen, J (1989) *The On-Site Costs of Soil Erosion in Mali* Environment Department Working Paper No 21, World Bank, Washington DC, November

incomes will generally be more complex than this. For example, yield reductions would reduce the requirement for weeding and harvesting. The Mali study allowed for these effects by looking at the total impact on farm budgets with and without erosion (see box).

The procedure described is an example of a 'dose-response' approach to valuation. The 'dose' is soil erosion, the 'response' is crop loss. Another approach would be to look at the costs of replacing the nutrients that are lost with soil erosion. Nutrient losses can be replaced with chemical fertilisers which have explicit market values.

Where it is not possible to engage in detailed assessment of the costs of resource degradation it is still useful to obtain 'best guess' calculations. In Burkina Faso estimates were made of the total amount of biomass lost each year in the form of fuelwood and vegetation. The resulting losses show up as forgone household energy (fuelwood) which can be valued at market prices for fuelwood; forgone millet and sorghum crops which can be valued at market prices; and reduced livestock yield due to fodder losses. Fuelwood losses amount to some CFAF 47 billion, livestock a further CFAF 10 billion, and cereal losses a further CFAF 15 billion. The grand total amounts to some 9% of Burkina Faso's GNP. It cannot be deduced from this that Burkina Faso's GNP is 9% less than it otherwise would be. This is because resources would have to be expended in order to rehabilitate eroded areas and to prevent further damage. But if the resources required are small, then the 9% figure is a ballpark estimate of the direct loss to Burkina Faso.

Provided they are credible, national environmental damage cost estimates can play a useful role in assessing development priorities. Because environmental damage costs do not show up explicitly in measures of national product, planners have no obvious incentive to treat environmental damage as a priority in development plans. Increasingly, however, environment is entering into development plans as the GNP costs of degradation are being shown to be significant and sometimes very substantial (see following box). Arguments of this kind are particularly appropriate at the level of macroeconomic management of the economy: it may be more important that the Ministry of Finance appreciates the costs of environmental degradation than that the Ministry of the Environment does.

The idea that economies 'lose' GNP because of environmental degradation is not straightforward. Some economists would argue along the following lines. All countries have 'developed' through

ESTIMATES OF NATIONAL ENVIRONMENTAL DAMAGE

Table 3 *The effects of global warming on food consumers and producers*

Country	δ_N	Air pollution	Water pollution	Coastal fisheries	Deforestation	Soil erosion	Change stocks of gas, oil, minerals etc	Others
					Composition of δ_N			
Brazil	9.8		0.1		8.7		1.0	
Burkina Faso	8.8				5.7	3.1		
Costa Rica	8.3			0.2	6.9	1.2		
Czechoslovakia	7.0							
Ethiopia	9.0				9.0			
Finland	1.6	1.6						
Germany (pre-unif.)	4.4	3.3	0.1					1.0
Hungary	5.0	5.0						
Indonesia	18.0			12.4	5.1	0.5		
Japan	2.4	0.9	0.5					1.0
Madagascar	15.4				11.7	2.3		1.4
Malawi	4.0					4.0		
Mali	6.0					6.0		
Mexico	12.0	3.0	1.0		5.0	1.0	2.0	
Netherlands	0.8	0.5	0.2					
Nigeria	17.4		10.2		2.6	3.4		0.1
Papua New Guinea	7.0							2.2
Philippines	4.0							
Poland	2.5	1.5	1.0					
USA	3.6	3.1	0.5					
Zimbabwe	4.8	0.9					3.9	

Table 3 shows estimates of the money value of environmental damage, or natural asset depreciation, in selected countries and according to the type of damage. Estimates are expressed as percentages of conventional GNP.

While the estimates use different techniques, relate to different years and vary in the quality of the underlying research, they suggest some broad interpretations. In the developed world total gross environmental damage may be around 2-4% of GNP; in the East European countries perhaps 5-10% of GNP; and in the poor developing nations perhaps 10% and above. This does not mean it is *worth* avoiding all this damage. Conservation costs resources as well. But since many conservation measures involve the removal of economic distortions (such as price controls, subsidies, undefined resource rights) the costs of conservation will, in many cases, be low.

Source: Pearce, D W and Atkinson, G (1992) *Are National Economies Sustainable? Measuring Sustainable Development* Centre for Social and Economic Research on the Global Environment, University College London

processes which have as their incidental effect the loss of environmental quality and environmental assets. The United Kingdom, for example, experienced horrendous air and water pollution during the industrial revolution. Arguably, the poor environmental quality was a price that had to be paid in order to secure that economic development. Indeed, it may even be the case that the loss of environmental assets is what triggers the development process, or part of it. Great Britain deforested much of its land because of the demand for fuelwood, the pressure to convert land to other uses, and the industrial demand for wood. This in turn helped force the search for other energy sources such as coal and, eventually, coke made from coal. These energy sources were the basis of the industrial revolution.

If this story is credible, it may be that the 5, 10 or even 20% losses of GNP being estimated by economic valuation procedures are illusory. The rest of the GNP is actually *higher* than it would have been had these environmental assets not been degraded. This is an appealing view for those who find environmentalists' concerns rather irritating and unworldly (and this group includes quite a few economists). But it is deeply flawed.

First, it is not even correct as a reflection on history. Some societies have actually disappeared because they ran out of accessible natural resources. Had natural resource scarcity been the spur to development at all times, this would not be true. While the Romans sought expanding colonies partly to secure their wood supplies, the great civilisation of Knossos declined because of their absence. The reality is that there has to be some other resource for people to turn to if one resource runs out. For Mali, Ethiopia and Burkina Faso, for example, no other resource is obvious.

Second, for the somewhat Panglossian view that 'environmental degradation is good in the long term' to hold, we have to be assured that the degradation is necessary. That is, either development would not take place without the degradation, or at least the benefits of degradation are less than the costs. Advocates of the long benefits of degradation do not offer evidence on costs and benefits but they are frequently the same people who argue that the prime cause of degradation is economic distortions in the form of subsidies to agricultural inputs, or controls on agricultural output prices. But the two views cannot be held simultaneously. If economic distortions are the main cause of environmental degradation, then not only is it socially beneficial to remove the distortions (otherwise they would not be called distortions in the first place), but it is environmentally beneficial as well. Environmental degradation becomes the result of misguided economic policies, not a necessary part of some economic evolutionary process by which development is achieved.

Those who argue that environmental degradation is a cycle in a long-term trend towards 'development' really have very little to substantiate their view. They would have at least a credible argument if the proceeds of natural resource degradation were invested in other forms of capital of a more productive nature. But the world is full of countries that have consumed the proceeds of resource depreciation as the science of 'green national accounting' is increasingly showing (see below). Nor is the process of environmental capital consumption confined to poor countries. Oil-rich states like the Netherlands and the United Kingdom have also been guilty.

Modifying the national accounts

Macroeconomic management makes extensive use of the *national economic accounts* which record monetary flows and transactions within the economy. The primary purpose of the accounts is to record economic activity, not to measure aggregate well-being in the nation. None the less, national accounts are widely used to indicate well-being, and rates of change in national aggregates such as GNP are widely construed as measures of 'development'. Whether the accounts are designed to record economic activity or measure well-being, or both, they are deficient in respect of their treatment of environment. Economic activity involves the use of materials and energy, and, once transformed into products, those same resources become, sooner or later, waste products. Any measure of economic activity which ignores these materials and energy flows will fail to record important activities which affect the *sustainability* of the economic activity. In the same way, any measure of well-being which ignores the resource and energy flows will fail to measure *sustainable well-being*. For these reasons, there is no widespread consensus that the national accounts need to be modified at least with respect to the way in which environmental 'stocks' and 'flows' are recorded.

Material and energy flows begin at the point of extraction, harvest or use of natural resources. They end by being waste products, ie emissions to ambient environments, discharges to water, and solid waste to land or sea. Logically, then, GNP needs to be modified to account for:

- any depreciation of natural capital stocks, in the same way that *net* national income is equal to gross national income *less* estimated depreciation on man-made capital. This is a measure of the 'draw down' of natural capital;
- any damage losses accruing to human wellbeing from the extraction, processing and disposal of materials and energy to receiving environments.

Both adjustments involve *economic valuation*. Indeed, it is somewhat ironic that many of the critics of economic valuation are also advocates of measures of 'green GNP', seemingly unaware that we cannot compute green GNP without economic valuation of environmental change! The first adjustment involves a valuation of the natural capital stock, the second involves valuation of such things as health impairment, pollution damage to buildings, crops and trees, aesthetic and recreational losses and other forms of 'psychic' damage. National accountants are not agreed on how best to make the appropriate adjustments. At the very least one form of adjustment to *gross* measures of national income would be:

Modified GNP = Conventional GNP + Value of environmental
services – Value of environmental damage.

In this way, additions to, say, national parks or improvements in pollution levels would be reflected in positive entries for modified GNP, and damage done would enter negatively. The way in which damage done should be measured is disputed. Some experts measure it by the expenditures necessary to offset the damage – the so-called *defensive expenditures*. Others wish to measure it using the kinds of valuation techniques which attempt to elicit *willingness to pay* to avoid damage or to improve environmental quality. Under certain circumstances it happens that defensive expenditures are perfect measures of WTP, but the use of defensive expenditures generally to measure damage done is strongly disputed in the national accounting literature. Moreover, defensive expenditures include both final and intermediate expenditures, breaking the equivalence between factor incomes and expenditures which is fundamental to conventional national accounting. Defensive expenditures by firms tend to be intermediate expenditures, whilst those by households are final expenditures. It is significant that the literature showing how expenditures can be perfect measures of WTP relates only to the household context.

Depreciation on stocks of natural capital also requires valuation and is relevant if the interest is in some measure of *sustainable income*, the income that a nation can receive without running down its capital base. In the conventional accounts this is partly accounted for by estimating *net national product* (NNP) which is defined as:

$$NNP = GNP - D_k$$

where D_k is the depreciation on man-made capital (machines, roads, buildings etc). The further adjustment that is required is:

$$NNP = GNP - D_k - D_n$$

where D_n is the depreciation of environmental assets.

The box below illustrates both types of adjustment, ie deducting environmental costs from GNP, and estimating the depreciation on

---

MODIFIED NATIONAL ACCOUNTS: AGRICULTURE AND FORESTRY IN THE UNITED KINGDOM

Provisional but non-official adjustments have been made to one sector of the UK's national accounts: agriculture and forestry. In line with the requirement that positive environmental effects (benefits) be added to GNP for this sector and that negative effects are deducted, the following adjustments can be made.

UK £million (1988)

Final marketed output		11,161
– Inputs	–	5,663
= Gross product	=	5,498
– Depreciation	–	1,470
= Net product	=	4,028
+ Environmental services		
biodiversity	+	94
amenity: green belt	+	642
amenity: nat. parks	+	152
– Government expenditure to maintain landscape and conserved areas, clean-up pollution	–	58
– Household defensive expenditures	–	na
– Depreciation (D_n)		
carbon fixing	+	146
water	–	11
= Sustainable net product	=	<4993

To make the adjustments to net product, estimates were made of the per hectare recreational and amenity values obtained from sample valuation studies. These were then applied to the whole area under conservation designations of one form or another. Willingness to pay to avoid damage was not estimated directly. The defensive expenditure approach was used, omitting companies' expenditure and including government anti-pollution expenditures. No estimates were available for household expenditures. Natural capital depreciation involved estimates for the net accretion or release of carbon dioxide and the valuation of water pollution. Because this sector has a net fixation rate of CO_2 this item appears positive in the adjustments. If household expenditures can be ignored, then the sector's accounts show an upwards revaluation by 24%, a significant adjustment.

Source: Adger, N and Whitby, M (1991) 'Land Use Externalities in National Accounting' in J Krabbe and W Heijman (eds) *National Income and Nature: Externalities, Growth and Steady State* Kluwer, Dordrecht, pp 77–101; and Adger, N and Whitby, M (1993) 'Natural Resource Accounting in the Land Use Sector: Theory and Practice' *European Review of Agricultural Economics*, vol 20, no 1

natural capital stocks. However the debate about modified national accounts develops, there is a clear role for economic valuation.

Setting national and sectoral priorities

Information on the economic value of policy changes can greatly assist the governmental process of setting policy and sectoral priorities. Estimating damage or benefit figures alone will not be sufficient for this process. It is necessary to compare the benefits of policy with the costs of policy. The presence of net benefits is sufficient to establish that existing or planned policy is *potentially* worthwhile, though not sufficient to establish that resources devoted to that end would not be better used elsewhere (net benefits may be greater still if the resources were put to an alternative use). But if benefits are less than costs then it can at least be inferred that resources should not be devoted on such a scale to the particular goal. This general requirement to review sectoral priorities in terms of benefits and costs has perhaps even greater force in the developing world where government income is at a premium. Indeed, this has always been one of the motives underlying the development of cost and benefit valuation techniques for developing countries. Despite this, sectoral benefit-cost techniques have been used in fairly limited ways in the developed world, and hardly at all in the developing world. Although there are a great many benefit-cost studies of specific policies in both developed and developing countries, few exist for establishing the worth of overall sectoral expenditures. The few attempts, however, have been revealing.

United States air pollution regulations probably cost some $13–14 billion in the single year 1981. Beyond that, annual costs probably rose fairly fast as standards were better and more extensively enforced and regulations grew in number. Benefits in 1978 were probably around $37 billion, and a little above this in 1981. Thus, for 1981, the overall air pollution control policy almost certainly yielded net social benefits. With a benefit-cost ratio of nearly 3, the regulations would seem to have been eminently worthwhile and it is unlikely that the resources involved would have yielded higher returns elsewhere. That conclusion needs to be qualified in several ways.

First, what was probably true of 1981 may not be true of years after that, especially as regulatory costs probably rose faster than benefits. Second, the conclusion assumes that all the improvements in US air quality in 1978 were due to prior legislation. In practice, as evidence from a number of countries shows, underlying structural changes in the economy have also contributed to improved air quality: eg switches from polluting fuels to less polluting ones due to ordinary market forces, reductions in heavy industry in favour of lighter, less polluting industry, changed consumer habits, and so on. Third, the picture changes somewhat if the regulatory policy is looked at in parts. It seems likely, for example, that 1970s US policy on air pollution from stationary sources did achieve net benefits, but policy on mobile sources (vehicles) probably generated net *costs*. A similar result emerges for federal water pollution policy. Costs of around $20–30 billion for 1985 compare to a best estimate of benefits of only some $14 billion. Not too much can be derived from such comparisons, but the results for mobile air pollution sources and for water pollution suggest the need to look carefully at the costs of policy. It has to be borne in mind, for example, that the costs quoted are estimates of the actual costs involved, not the costs that could have been involved if the most efficient policies had been pursued. One of the attractions of market-based approaches (taxes, charges, tradeable quotas and permits) is that they have the potential to keep compliance costs down. Savings may well be large, of a factor of two or more compared to the costs of traditional 'command-and-control' costs (see Portney, 1990).

In the real world of political decision-making, priorities are rarely set by reference to measures of costs and benefits. The greatest influence over policy is in the United States. Outside the USA very little actual influence has been exerted by cost-benefit analysis (Barde and Pearce, 1991). In part this reflects lack of understanding of the techniques involved, but in part it reflects the fact that decision-makers have multiple criteria for deciding on policies (nor, of course, are policies necessarily chosen on a rational basis from the social standpoint: chance, favouritism, patronage, whim and corruption are just as important). Benefit and damage estimation are therefore likely to be *part* of a wider package of criteria including distributional concerns, human health, and concerns over the quality of environmental impact and the sustainability of resource use. The following box illustrates one possible ranking of environmental issues in Nigeria according to various criteria.

Project, programme and policy evaluation

The traditional role for environmental damage and benefit estimation is

SETTING ENVIRONMENTAL PRIORITIES IN NIGERIA

To rank environmental priorities in order to obtain guidance for development aid to Nigeria, the World Bank adopted the following criteria:

- impact of environmental degradation on GNP;
- size of population affected by the environmental issue;
- incidence by income group of the degradation;
- a measure of resource integrity based on the relationship between waste (W) and environmental assimilative capacity (A); and
- a similar measure of resource integrity based on a comparison of harvest and use rates (H) compared to regeneration rates (R) for renewable resources.

The results are shown below (figures in square brackets are indicative only). While the data are clearly imperfect, the approach yields some coherent priorities. for example, soil degradation, deforestation and water pollution all rank 'high' on each of the general criteria of GNP impact, distributional incidence and resource integrity. Such rankings can assist national priority setting.

Table 4 *Ranking environmental priorities in Nigeria*

Issue	GNP loss $m/year	Population at risk (millions)	Social incidence (higher nos.=worse)	W > A	H > R
Soil degradation	3000+	50	2–3	3	3–4
Water pollution	1000+	40+	3–4	3–4	[3]
Deforestation	750+	50	2–3	[2]	4
Coastal erosion	c.150	<3	3	2–3	2
Gully erosion	c.100	<10	2–3	2	2
Fish loss	c. 50	<5	3	na	na
Wildlife	c. 10	<1	2	na	4
Air pollution	na	35	4	2–3	[1]
Water hyacinth	c. 50	5	2–3	2–3	na

Source: World Bank

in project appraisal. The main manuals that have influenced theoretical and practical work in *economic* project assessment have not, however, addressed environmental issues. Issues relating to the treatment of environmental factors are not, for example, discussed at all in the main project appraisal technical manuals (see Little and Mirrlees, 1974; Squire and van der Tak, 1975; Dasgupta et al, 1972; Gittinger, 1982). In contrast, assessing environmental impacts has been the subject of a wholly separate set of procedures known as *Environmental Impact Assessment* (EIA). EIA is important in drawing decision-makers' attention to the many forms of environmental impact. To some extent EIA also permits an assessment of the importance of impacts. The main problem, however, is that EIA tends to be pursued either as an adjunct to conventional economic appraisal, or as a precursor. In neither case is EIA *integrated* into economic appraisal. Yet comprehensive benefit-cost assessments require EIA to be carried out if they are to be truly comprehensive, accounting for environmental impacts.

Extending project appraisal to account for environmental impacts, or to the assessment of purely conservation projects, presents no conceptual problem for benefit-cost approaches. The typical benefit-cost assessment (BCA) calculates measured benefits and costs and converts them into an *economic rate of return* (ERR). In this process, market prices are adjusted for distortions, ie economic values are used (shadow prices). Environmental impacts are simply additional costs or benefits. The necessity for shadow pricing them tends to arise more from the fact that they lack associated markets altogether rather than from the existence of distorted markets. Indeed, economic valuation of environmental impacts is essentially a matter of shadow pricing. In order to focus on the environment, the traditional BCA rule for the potential acceptance of a project can be re-expressed as:

$$\Sigma_t \, (B_t - C_t - E_t) \times (1 + r)^{-t} > 0$$

where B_t is non-environmental benefit at time t, C is non-environmental cost, r is the discount rate, and E is environmental cost (and the sign would be positive for environmental benefits). Economic valuation is concerned with the monetary measurement of E in this inequality. Environmental issues do, however, raise a further problem, namely the selection of r, the discount rate, in the above inequality.

Projects
The following box shows how project economic rates of return can be

RATES OF RETURN TO AFFORESTATION IN NORTHERN NIGERIA

Careful examination and measurement of the environmental benefits of afforestation can greatly increase the 'economic rate of return' to forestry investments. One study assessed the benefits of afforestation in northern Nigeria as:

- halting the future decline of soil fertility (since trees typically reduce soil erosion);
- raising current levels of soil fertility;
- producing tree products – fuelwood, poles, fruits; and
- producing fodder both from raised productivity of soils and from forest fodder.

The net present values (NPVs) and economic rates of return (ERRs) that resulted for shelterbelts (planting trees mainly for wind protection) and farm forestry (intermixing trees and crops) were as shown in Table 5.

Table 5 *Impacts of afforestation in northern Nigeria*

| | Shelterbelts | | Farm forestry | |
	NPV	IRR	NPV	IRR
Base case	170	14.9	129	19.1
Low yield, high cost	110	13.1	70	14.5
High yield	221	16.2	–	–
No erosion	108	13.5	75	16.6
More rapid erosion	109	13.6	60	15.5
Soil restored + yield jump	263	16.9	203	21.8
Wood benefits only (*)	–95	4.7	–14	7.4

(* wood and fruit for farm forestry)

Calculation of timber costs and benefits alone in the Kano area have tended to show rates of return of around 5%, which has to be compared with the cut-off rate which is usually much higher, at around 10%. In other words, afforestation does not pay. But once the other benefits are included, dramatic increases in rates of return can be secured.

The analysis shows that counting 'wood benefits' only produces negative net present value and correspondingly low economic rates of return. But if allowance is made for the effects of trees on crop yields, and for expected rates of soil erosion in the absence of afforestation, the picture is transformed for both farm forestry and shelterbelts.

Source: Anderson, D (1987) *The Economics of Afforestation: a Case Study in Africa* Johns
Hopkins University Press, Baltimore; and Anderson, D (1989) 'Economic Aspects of
Afforestation and Soil Conservation Projects' in G Schramm and J Warford
Environmental Management and Economic Development Johns Hopkins University
Press, Baltimore, pp 172–184

transformed when due account is taken of the detailed environmental
consequences of planting trees. The analysis makes extensive use of
data on the various *physical interlinkages* in environmental and
agricultural systems. Trees have many functions, for example, from
producing timber for poles, to fuelwood supply, leaves for animal
fodder, crop wind protection and, in some cases, the fixing of ambient
nitrogen. The principles of benefit–cost analysis (BCA) require that *all*
impacts be accounted for.

Programmes

Just as project appraisal requires comprehensive environmental valuation so, logically, does *programme* appraisal. Programmes tend to be
amalgams of often interrelated projects, policy measures and development plans. As with single projects, the environmental implications of
a programme should be evaluated, and the overall return to the
programme should be assessed with reference to the inclusion of
environmental enhancement components – tree planting, soil conservation, water supply etc. In programme analysis, environmental rates of
return (ERRs) should still be estimated wherever possible, especially
where the intermixing of policy changes and projects is liable to make
ERRs higher than if projects alone were being evaluated. The box on
page 17 illustrates some of the kinds of benefits from environmental
conservation in a tropical forest context.

Choice of technology

Within a programme the issue of *choice of technology* usually arises. A
given development objective may be met by selecting from a range of
technological options. The programme objective of meeting a given
increment in electricity demand, for example, involves selection of
incremental electric power sources which contribute to the overall
objective of meeting demand at *least cost*. Whereas least cost power
system planning has typically been couched in terms of the *private* costs
of generation and distribution, environmental considerations require
that the criterion be modified to become least *social* cost, ie inclusive of

the environmental impacts of different energy technologies. In some developed economies this redefinition has resulted in the estimation of 'externality adders'. These are the surcharges or credits to be attached to specific energy technologies according to their relative environmental impacts. Expressed in this way, the credits and debits have to be measured in money terms, so that it is the monetary value of

EXTERNALITY ADDERS FOR ELECTRICITY GENERATION SYSTEMS IN THE USA

Many economists advocate the use of 'adders' to the ruling prices of electricity in order to reflect better the true costs of electricity production and consumption. Environmental adders would reflect the damage done to the environment. One study has made the following calculations. The surcharges are calculated according to the monetary value of impacts relating to sulphur dioxide, nitrogen dioxide, carbon dioxide and particulate emissions. Nuclear power costs are based on the value of damage done by routine emissions, accidents and the costs of decommissioning.

Table 6 *Environmental surcharges for electricity in the USA*

Electricity technology	Surcharge (USc/kWh generated)
Coal	
Conventional	0.058
Fluidised bed combustion	0.028
Integrated gas combined cycle	0.025
Oil	
Low sulphur	0.027
High sulphur	0.067
Natural gas	
Steam plant	0.010
Combined cycle	0.010
Nuclear power	
Routine emissions	0.110
Accidents	2.300
Decommissioning	0.500
Nuclear total:	2.910

For this particular study, the rankings would be (in order of most damaging to least damaging) nuclear power, oil, coal and gas. This is probably in accord with public perception for the developed world. The very high penalty to nuclear power is seen to be largely a function of the estimated accident costs. In terms of *new* plant choice, therefore, the relevance of this penalty would depend on modifications to safety designs which would affect risk factors.

Source: Ottinger, R et al (1990) *Environmental Costs of Electricity*, PACE University Center for Environmental Legal Studies, White Plains, New York, September

environmental impacts that is used to calculate the price adjustments. The box above illustrates the kinds of calculation that are involved. The 'adders' are then added to or subtracted from the private costs of generation. As an illustration, nuclear power might be credited with avoiding carbon dioxide and acid rain emissions, but it would be debited with a surcharge for any routine or accidental radiation risks. Several countries are experimenting with the estimation of externality adders. If applied in practice, choice of energy technologies in a least-cost planning system could change markedly.

The Polluter Pays Principle

The externality addition approach extends beyond choice of technology. Existing sources of supply and service can be priced to reflect environmental damage, as the general principles of optimal resource allocation would require. Adding surcharges in this way is consistent with the *Polluter Pays Principle* (PPP) which OECD member countries subscribe to (see box). The PPP requires that those emitting damaging wastes to the environment should bear the costs of avoiding that damage or of containing the damage to within acceptable limits according to national environmental standards. As stated, the PPP does *not* require that environmental damage be valued in monetary terms, although it could be. Whatever the cost of achieving the national standard, that cost should, in the first instance, be borne by the emitter of waste. That the emitter's increased costs may then be passed on partly to the consumer is still consistent with the PPP. The costs borne by the emitter and the consumer can be thought of as a form of valuation. Regulatory agencies set standards on behalf of the voting population, and the cost of meeting those standards becomes, effectively, a minimum estimate of what the regulator regards the damage to

---

THE POLLUTER PAYS PRINCIPLE

The following is the statement by the OECD of the Polluter Pays Principle (emphasis added).

1　Environmental resources are in general limited and their use in production and consumption activities may lead to their deterioration. *When the cost of this deterioration is not adequately taken into account in the price system, the market fails to reflect the scarcity of such resources both at the national and international levels.* Public measures are thus necessary to reduce pollution and to reach a better allocation of resources by ensuring that prices of goods depending on the quality and/or quantity of environmental resources reflect more closely their relative scarcity and that economic agents concerned react accordingly.

2　In many circumstances, in order to ensure that the environment is in an acceptable state, the reduction of pollution beyond a certain level will not be practical or even necessary in view of the costs involved.

3　The principle to be used for allocating costs of pollution prevention and control measures to encourage rational use of scarce environmental resources and to avoid distortions in international trade and investment is the so-called 'Polluter Pays Principle'. This principle means that the environment is in an acceptable state. In other words, *the cost of these measures should be reflected in the costs of goods and services which cause pollution in production and/or consumption.* Such measures should not be accompanied by subsidies that would create significant distortions in international trade and investment.

4　This principle should be an objective of member countries; however, there may be exceptions or special arrangements, particularly for the transitional periods, provided that they do not lead to significant distortions in international trade and investment.

Source: OECD (1975) *The Polluter Pays Principle: Definition, Analysis, Implementation* OECD, Paris

---

be. Nor is it essential for the general PPP to be implemented via taxation or some other form of 'economic instrument' (tradeable permit, product charge, tax-subsidy etc). The PPP is consistent with traditional standard setting via 'command and control' policies.

None the less, economic instruments have many attractions over command and control policies. If this approach is used then it is fundamental to their use that any charge or tax should be at least proportional to damage done. Valuation therefore becomes important in giving guidance to the setting of such environmental prices. The following box shows how a tax on greenhouse gases might be computed using the economic valuation of global warming damage as a base. The analysis suggests that, if global warming produces an impact on global national product, or what we might call global world product (GWP),

---

DERIVING A CARBON TAX FROM GLOBAL WARMING DAMAGE ESTIMATES

Several studies have attempted to calculate the monetary value of damage from global warming. Estimates are highly uncertain but can be expected to improve as the underlying physical data and global circulation models improve. Nordhaus estimates that damage might amount to some 1% of gross world product (GWP) expressed in present value terms. Comparing this to the probable costs of reducing greenhouse gas emissions, he estimates that the reduction in gases that would bring the greatest net benefit to the world would be some 11% off a baseline trend of projected emissions. The table below shows the cost and benefit comparison.

Table 7 *Costs and benefits of reducing global warming*

% Greenhouse gas emission reduction (%)	Total cost of reduction ($b)	Total benefit of reduction ($b)	Net total benefits ($b)
1	0.04	0.60	0.56
2	0.12	1.20	1.08
3	0.24	1.80	1.56
4	0.40	2.30	1.90
5	0.61	2.90	2.39
10	2.20	5.90	3.70
11	2.90	6.40	3.50
15	6.80	8.80	2.00
25	30.70	14.70	-16.00

The estimates suggest that greenhouse gases – aggregated and measured in terms of CO_2-equivalent – should be reduced in aggregate by a little over 10%. To find the surcharge necessary to achieve this optimal reduction, it is necessary to calculate the extra damage done by each extra ton of CO_2-equivalent. This is $7.30 per ton CO_2-equivalent for the damage costs shown.

But it would rise to $66 per ton if damages were twice the estimated level – corresponding to 2% of GWP.

These estimates are open to many reservations. If it is comparatively easy to control emissions, then the costs of control may be less than shown, dictating a higher optimal level of greenhouse gas reduction. If there are, as many scientists believe, certain thresholds beyond which damage would become very severe, then the benefit estimates would rise, and also justify stricter controls. Certainly, those countries that are committed to greenhouse gas controls, over and above those for chlorofluorocarbons, are talking about far more extensive levels of control.

Source for data: Nordhaus, W (1991) 'A Sketch of the Economics of the Greenhouse Effect' *American Economic Review*, vol 81, no 2, pp 146–150

of around 1%, then a very modest 'carbon tax' of about $7 per ton of CO_2-equivalent would secure the optimal reduction of greenhouse gas emissions of about 10%. But if damage rises to 2% of GWP, then the tax is above $60 per ton. Taxes computed so that they secure the level of pollution reduction that yields the greatest net benefits are 'optimal pollution taxes' and are special examples of the PPP.

Policies

Policy changes can also be evaluated using the benefit-cost framework with special reference to environmental implications. The costs of implementing the policy can be compared with the benefits obtained from it. The following box shows the computations used to determine whether or not the Environmental Protection Agency (EPA) would recommend reducing lead in gasoline in the USA.

Economic valuation and sustainable development

The need for economic valuation of environmental impacts and of environmental assets arises quite independently of the definition of sustainable development. Simply pursuing *efficient* policies and investing in *efficient* projects and programmes requires valuation to be pursued as long as it is credible. At the most general level of intergenerational concern, valuation is still required. If transfers of resources are to be made between generations – with the current generation sacrificing for the future, or future benefits being lost for the sake of present gain – then it is essential to know *what* is being sacrificed and *how much* it is that is being surrendered. It is not necessary,

THE USE OF BENEFIT-COST ANALYSIS IN DECISION MAKING: LEAD IN GASOLINE

Under Executive Order 12291 of 1981 in the USA, government agencies were required to use 'Regulatory Impact Analysis' (RIA) and to adopt regulatory processes that would maximise 'the net benefits to society'. The Order was the first to establish the net benefit objective as the criterion for adopting regulatory processes, although its adoption has been circumscribed by existing laws relating to other objectives.

Benefit-cost analysis played an important role in the adoption of regulations concerning lead in gasoline. Ambient lead concentrations were thought to be linked to serious health effects, including retardation, kidney disease and even death. The Environmental Protection Agency conducted a benefit-cost study with the results shown below.

The regulation involved reducing lead in gasoline from 1.1 grams per gallon (gpg) to 0.1 gpg. The costs of the rule are shown as 'total refining costs'. Refinery costs increase because lead has traditionally been used to boost octane levels in fuel, and other means would have to be found to achieve this. The benefits included:

- improved children's health;
- improved blood pressure in adults;
- reduced damages from misfuelled vehicles, arising from hydrocarbon, NO_x and CO emissions; and
- impacts on maintenance and fuel economy.

Children's health

The EPA study found that blood lead levels closely tracked trends in gasoline lead. Medical costs for the care of children would be reduced by reducing lead concentrations, and there would be less need for compensatory education for IQ-impaired children. These savings are shown as 'children's health effects' in Table 8.

Adult blood pressure

Blood lead levels were thought to be associated with blood pressure and hypertension. Medical costs would be saved if these illnesses could be reduced. Moreover, some heart attacks and strokes would be avoided. A value of a 'statistical life' of $1 million was used for the latter. The resulting values show up in the 'adult blood pressure' row of Table 8. They are seen to be high because of the involvement of mortality-avoidance in this benefit.

Other pollutants

Reducing lead in gasoline also reduces other pollutants. This is because making unleaded fuel the 'norm' reduces the risk of 'misfuelling', ie using leaded fuels in vehicles designed for unleaded fuels. The mechanism whereby misfuelling is reduced is through the higher cost of leaded fuels at the new low-lead concentration. This deters drivers from purchasing the leaded fuel. As misfuelling is reduced, so emissions of HC, NO_x and CO are reduced. Damage done by these pollutants was estimated by studies of ozone pollution damage (ozone arises from HC and CO emissions), but estimates were also made of the value of the equipment destroyed by misfuelling. The figures appearing in the row 'conventional pollutants' in the table are in fact an average of the two methods.

Table 8 *Reducing lead in gasoline: costs and benefits, USA, 1985-92*

	1985	1986	1987	1988	1989	1990	1991	1992
MONETIZED BENEFITS ($m 1983)								
Children's health effects	223	600	547	502	453	414	369	358
Adult blood pressure	1724	5897	5675	5447	5187	4966	4682	4691
Conventional pollutants	0	222	222	224	226	230	239	248
Maintenance	102	914	859	818	788	767	754	749
Fuel economy	35	187	170	113	134	139	172	164
TOTAL MONETIZED BENEFITS	2084	7820	7473	7104	6788	6516	6216	6210
TOTAL REFINING COSTS	96	608	558	532	504	471	444	441
NET BENEFITS	1988	7212	6915	6573	6284	6045	5772	5769
NET BENEFITS EXCLUDING BLOOD PRESSURE	264	1315	1241	1125	1097	1079	1090	1078

Maintenance and fuel economy

Maintenance costs for vehicles were expected to fall due to reduced corrosive effects of lead and its scavengers on engines and exhaust systems. Fewer engine tune-ups and oil changes would be needed, exhaust systems would last longer. Fuel economy was expected to rise as the new technologies to raise octane levels to what they were previously also increases the energy content of fuels. There would also be reduced fouling of oxygen sensors. Maintenance benefits outweighed fuel economy benefits by around 6 to 1. The totals are shown in the table.

The net benefits from reducing lead in gasoline are seen to be substantial, even if the blood pressure benefits (which dominate the aggregate benefits) are excluded. Indeed, it can be seen that the regulation would be worthwhile *even if all health benefits are excluded*. In the event, the blood pressure benefits were excluded from the final decision because the research establishing this link was judged too recent to permit adequate review. The lead regulation was also of interest because of the introduction of a 'lead permits system' to reduce the financial burden on the refining industry. Essentially, this allowed 'lead quotas' to be traded between refiners. Refiners who found it easy to get below the limit were allowed to sell their 'surplus' lead rights to refiners who found it expensive to get back to desirable octane levels without lead. The particular feature of the lead-in-gasoline benefit-cost study that made it a powerful aid to decision-making was the clear-cut nature of the net benefits even when uncertainties about benefits were allowed for. But it was also executed carefully and in comprehensive detail.

Source: US Environmental Protection Agency (1987) *EPA's Use of Benefit-Cost Analysis 1981–1986* EPA-230-05-87-028, Washington DC, August; and US EPA (1985) *Costs and Benefits of Reducing Lead in Gasoline: Final Regulatory Impact Analysis* EPA-230-05-85-006, Washington DC, February

therefore, to invoke the philosophy of sustainable development, however it is defined, to justify a focus on economic valuation in a development context.

However, if one or more definitions of sustainable development are to be espoused, the role of economic valuation needs to be investigated. An efficient use of resources need not be a sustainable one. The optimal rate at which an exhaustible resource should be depleted, for example, still requires that the rate of use is positive. In the absence of repeated discoveries of further identical resources, the resource must be exhausted eventually. Every unit of use today is at the cost of a forgone unit tomorrow. Global warming is another example of an activity that impairs the welfare of future generations. 'Sustainability' therefore implies something about maintaining the level of human well-being so that it might improve but at least never declines (or, not more than temporarily, anyway). Interpreted this way, sustainable development becomes equivalent to some requirement that well-being does not decline through time. The implication for *valuation* is now somewhat different to what is implied by consideration of efficiency alone. It now becomes necessary to measure human well-being in order to establish that it does not decline through time, and since environmental assets contribute to well-being it is necessary to measure preferences for and against environmental change.

The problem from the point of view of development planning and aid is that a simple 'trends continued' cannot be *assumed*. This is particularly true if the environmental changes in question risk harming future well-being in any significant way. In terms of Figure 1, a development path such as A appears to be sustainable; B is non-

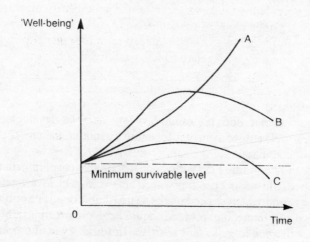

Figure 1 *Sustainable development paths*

sustainable (but could be 'efficient')' whilst C is both unsustainable and non-survivable because average well-being levels fall below some minimum level (eg a poverty line). But *from the vantage point of 0* in the diagram, it may not be possible to tell *which* development path a country is on. Hence, defining sustainable development as sustained well-being is of only limited help in real world development planning. Observing that the rate of growth of well-being is declining (path C) may be an early indicator, but that would not detect the unsustainability of path B. Moreover, A and B look very similar to begin with. What matters is knowing whether the *conditions* for sustainable development are fulfilled or not.

If the focus is on the conditions for achieving sustainable development, then it may be that wholly non-economic indicators will suffice. For example, computations of the *carrying capacity* of natural environments could act as early warnings of non-survivability (path C). Carrying capacity measures the number of people whose livelihoods can be sustained by a given stock of resources if each of them consumes the minimum level of those resources necessary to survive. If the numbers resulting are less than the actual population present then the situation appears to be non-survivable and therefore certainly non-sustainable. Carrying capacity indicators would need to be calculated on a regular basis for the measure to be useful in this context. Typically, carrying capacity measures are produced on an *ad hoc* basis and for a single year only. None the less they offer one anticipatory measure of sustainability. Other physical measures could include assessments of the rate of resource use relative to the rate of resource regeneration and the rate of waste emissions relative to the assimilative capacity of the environment. It may be therefore that some light will be shed on sustainability indicators by non-economic approaches, especially if they can be developed to include other measures of stress and shock to underlying natural resource systems.

The literature on environmental economics tends to suggest that the clues to sustainability lie in the quantity and quality of a nation's *capital stock*. Part of the intuition here is that nations are like corporations. No corporation would regard itself as sustainable if it used up its capital resources to fund its sales and profits expansion. As long as capital assets are at least intact, and preferably growing, any profit or income earned can be regarded as 'sustainable'. On this analogy nations are no different. Sustainable growth and development cannot be achieved if capital assets are declining. Indeed, some economic growth models suggest strongly that if capital assets are kept intact, one concept of intergenerational equity – that of equalising real consumption per capita – can be achieved providing population growth does not outstrip the rate of technological change. (This is an important proviso, since it is likely to be met in rich countries but not in the poorest countries).

If a condition for achieving sustainable development is that capital stocks be kept intact, then the problem of how to tell whether a nation is 'on' or 'off' a sustainable development path is partially resolved. It is not necessary to observe real levels of well-being as such, but instead to look at the underlying condition and amount of the capital stock. Unfortunately, while this approach solves one problem it raises many others. First, it is necessary to know what it is that counts as capital. Second, it has to be measurable, otherwise 'constancy' cannot be tested (constancy throughout should be read as 'constant or increasing').

The national accounting issue arises again in this context of defining and measuring capital. Capital assets in the national accounts are typically confined to 'man-made' capital – machines, roads, factories. Some accounts include some measure of mineral wealth as capital. The depreciation of the man-made capital is then deducted from GNP to give NNP. A more comprehensive definition of capital and income would include *human* capital (knowledge, skills etc) and *natural* capital (environmental assets). The primary condition for sustainable development would then be that this *aggregate* stock of capital should not decline. Put another way, depreciation on this capital stock should not exceed the rate of new investment in capital assets.

But how is the capital stock to be measured? For some economies heavily dependent on one or two natural resources it may be possible to use a physical indicator of reserves or available stocks. But for the vast majority, it will be necessary to find a measuring rod for capital. Typically that means money units – ie it becomes necessary to *value* capital, including environmental capital. Valuation and sustainable development are again intricately linked. How *far* this link matters depends in large part on how likely unsustainable development paths are, and, of course, on the value judgement that sustainability 'matters'. Opinions differ. *Past* development suggests that technological change and the expansion of human knowledge will make resource use more and more efficient with benefits to subsequent generations. Some technologies have, of course, brought their own damage costs (chlorofluorocarbons, for example): technology is not a free good. How far *future* development will be sustainable perhaps revolves round the issue of *irreversibility*. The more irreversible the damage done by the current generation, the fewer degrees of freedom future generations will have to expand their own well-being. Sustainable development certainly looks as if it should be partially guided by the need to avoid irreversibly significant damage.

If securing sustainable development has something to do with monitoring and measuring *aggregate* capital stocks and not allowing them to decline, then there need be no particular role for environmental protection in sustainable development. Environmental assets could decline in quantity as long as depreciation in these assets was offset by investment in other man-made assets or human capital. But even if this view of sustainability is accepted, then valuation is still central to the process. For it is not then possible to know whether offsetting investment has taken place unless there is some measure of the rate of depreciation on natural assets and their forgone economic rate of return. Still others will want to make a special case for the environment. The acceptability of 'running down' environmental assets provided other assets are built up will depend on relative valuations and judgements about other measures of sustainability, as well as on the moral view about destroying the environment.

The following box shows a possible empirical interpretation of the

---

MEASURING SUSTAINABLE DEVELOPMENT

An economy is sustainable if it saves more than the depreciation on its man-made and natural capital

Table 9 shows estimates of the proportion of savings to national income in selected economies; the amount of depreciation on man-made capital (as a percentage of income) and estimates of the depreciation and damage to natural resources and the environment (again expressed as a percentage of national income). If savings exceeds the sum of the two estimates of depreciation and damage, the economy is 'sustainable'. Otherwise it is not. The measure is crude and simplistic and the estimates of environmental damage are especially limited. But the analysis is suggestive. Those economies we might expect to be unsustainable, certainly are. Note that the rule used here is what we call 'weak sustainability' since it assumes that natural and man-made capital are perfect substitutes. Much of the literature on ecology teaches us that this is not true. A stricter, 'strong sustainability' measure may be preferred.

Table 9 *Sustainability of selected national economies*

Sustainable economies	S/Y	−	δ_M/Y	−	δ_N/Y	=	Z
Brazil	20		7		10		+ 3
Costa Rica	26		3		8		+15
Czechoslovakia	30		10		7		+13
Finland	28		15		2		+11
Germany (pre-unification)	26		12		4		+10
Hungary	26		10		5		+11
Japan	33		14		2		+17
Netherlands	25		10		1		+14
Poland	30		11		3		+16
USA	18		12		4		+ 2
Zimbabwe	24		10		5		+ 9
Marginally sustainable							
Mexico	24		12		12		0
Philippines	15		11		4		0
Unsustainable							
Burkina Faso	2		1		10		−9
Ethiopia	3		1		9		−7
Indonesia	20		5		17		−2
Madagascar	8		1		16		−9
Malawi	8		7		4		−3
Mali	−4		4		6		−14
Nigeria	15		3		17		−5
Papua New Guinea	15		9		7		−1

Note: S = national savings, Y = national income, δ_M = depreciation on man-made capital, δ_N = depreciation and damage to natural resources and the environment, Z = (weak) sustainability

Source: Pearce, D W and Atkinson, G (1992) *Are National Economies Sustainable? Measuring Sustainable Development* Centre for Social and Economic Research on the Global Environment (CSERGE), University College London

link between economic valuation and one approach to determining whether a country is on a sustainable development path. This approach is termed 'weak sustainability' and reflects the idea that a country needs to save more than the depreciation on its assets if it is to be judged sustainable. (Strictly, the rule is that it needs to save more than the sum of asset depreciation and the willingness to pay to avoid environmental damage – see Pearce and Atkinson, 1992). Writing the rule as:

$$S > Dm + Dn$$

where S is savings and Dm is 'depreciation' on man-made capital and Dn is depreciation and damage related to environmental assets, then we can use the measures of damage from the 'green GNP' studies to measure Dn. Estimates of S are readily available, and estimates of Dm exist for quite a number of countries. The approach is illustrative and the data are very imperfect. But the result is instructive. Countries that intuitively seem unsustainable turn out to be unsustainable. Recall that this is the 'weak' definition of sustainability. A stronger definition would require that there be no net damage to environmental assets overall, closer to the way many environmentalists (and ecological scientists) would see the world.

Discussing sustainable development in broad terms risks giving the impression that philosophers and economists fiddle while the Rome of under-development burns. But there is nothing in the ideas of sustainable development that lessens the emphasis on development now, or on targeting the most vulnerable. It will risk this if it is used to justify large sacrifices of real income and well-being now for very long term gains that are highly uncertain. Eliciting economic values can help guard against the latter risk by showing, as far as possible, where and when environmental protection yields the highest returns.

Chapter 3

Valuation and discounting the future

INTRODUCTION

Many environmental problems – nuclear waste storage, nuclear power station decommissioning, the release of long-lived micropollutants, ozone layer depletion, global warming – are likely to have their major impacts well into the future. The costs are therefore likely to be borne by people alive in 50 years time and after that. Conventional benefit-cost approaches would regard $1 of future damage as being less important that $1 of damage now because of the phenomenon of *discounting*. The underlying value judgements of benefit-cost analysis are that 'people's preferences count' and that preferences are justifiably weighted according to the existing distribution of incomes. If the sovereignty of preferences is to be applied consistently, then the bias of the preferences of the current generation towards present as opposed to future benefits, and against present as opposed to future costs, needs to be reflected in decision-making aids. This is the essential rationale for discounting. Typically, any benefit (or cost), B (or C), accruing in T years' time is recorded as having a 'present' value, PV, of:

$$PV(B) = \frac{B_T}{(1 + r)^T}$$

where r is the rate at which future benefits are discounted, the discount rate.

The problem that arises with discounting is that it *discriminates against future generations*. In one sense this discrimination is deliberate – the discount rate is *meant* to discriminate in this way, this is its purpose. But such a discrimination presupposes an agreed objective to the effect that meeting the current generation's wants is more important that meeting future generations' wants. Discounting is consistent with imposing a major cost on the future for the sake of a relatively small gain now. The usual justification for this is that future generations will be better off anyway – their incomes will be higher because of economic growth. They will therefore attach less value to an extra $1 of income than a current generation (the 'diminishing marginal utility of income' argument) and will perhaps be better placed to counteract any ill effects of current generation activities that spill over to them. To see the kind of implied shifting of burdens, a cost accruing in 100 years time and amounting to $100 billion would, at a 10 per cent discount rate, have a present value of

$$\frac{\$100 \text{ billion}}{(1.1)^{100}}$$

which comes to $7.25 *million*. That is, any benefit-cost study of a project imposing such a future cost would record the damage done at only $7.25 million even though the actual damage done is nearly 14,000 times greater than this. If there is concern with *intergenerational equity*, then, discount rates of the order of 10 per cent – which are typically applied to investments in the developing world – would be inconsistent with that concern.

ACCOUNTING FOR FUTURE GENERATIONS

Intergenerational concerns would therefore seem to call for some fairly fundamental revision in the way project and policy appraisal is carried out. Two broad categories of modification have been suggested, although it is as well to note that all the arguments are the subject of extended controversy. The first set of modifications requires what might be called a 'two tier' approach. Allocations of resources *over time* are treated differently to allocations *within* a period of time. Some kind of 'sustainability rule' is applied to the *intergenerational* allocation, and fairly conventional rules, such as maximising the net present value of benefits, are applied within a time-frame. The second set of modifications is made directly to the discount rate itself, ie the framework of maximising net present values is left intact, but the actual *rate* of discount is changed to reflect intergenerational concerns.

Sustainability criteria

Some authors argue that simply changing the discount rate – usually by lowering it – is a mistaken procedure because what is being done is to attempt to modify a procedure based on *efficiency* gains and losses for a major redefinition of the underlying objective – *intergenerational fairness*. On this argument, it should not be surprising to find that an issue of fairness cannot be handled by modifying efficiency criteria. Added to this, an appraisal procedure that evolved from concerns with mainly localised and certainly marginal changes to the state of the economy is being called upon to apply to issues that are global in a non-marginal sense, ie significant changes in well-being are involved. A tool for fine-tuning decisions is being applied to contexts where fine-tuning is not the issue. More fundamentally, transfers between generations should not be treated in the same way as decisions about how to use resources available to the current generation. Equity issues within a generation can be treated by making resource transfers between individuals. Equity issues between generations need to be treated the same way: pursuing efficiency within a generation does not guarantee a fair distribution of resources through time.

One way to avoid some of the concerns about discounting is to impose a *sustainability constraint*. Essentially, this amounts to formulating some rule which would maximise gains to well-being now provided this does not reduce the well-being of future generations below that of the current generation (very much in line with the Brundtland Commission definition of sustainable development). This is a departure from benefit-cost analysis because it requires well-being to be constant or increasing over time. Benefit-cost analysis would be consistent with reducing current well-being if it yields a greater benefit for future generations, and *vice versa*. Rules of this kind have been formulated in terms of maintaining overall stocks of capital of all kinds – man-made, human and natural. The basic idea is not to ensure equal (or rising) well-being through time, but equal or rising *capability* of generating well-being through time. The stock of capital is the means of raising well-being, and hence it is this stock that has to be maintained or improved.

In *practical* terms such rules would require monitoring and measurement of capital stocks and an investment policy that sought at all times to ensure that net investment offset depreciation ('compensating investments'). The main difficulties would lie in the issue of measuring capital since physical units would not be adequate due to the heterogeneity of capital (the 'adding up' problem). Hence a valuation procedure would be needed. Then either the total value of the capital stock would be monitored and adjusted so that it is constant or rising, or perhaps the *price* of the capital stock would be used as an indicator – resource prices, for example, would be monitored and demand and supply adjusted so as to secure constant real prices through time.

As yet little advance in this area has been made beyond the attempts to recompute GNP to reveal net investment levels that allow for depreciation on some natural capital assets. Such procedures are promising, but to be all-embracing they would have to be extended to all forms of non-marketed capital and especially environmental capital. At the global level substantial problems arise – some forms of capital will depreciate because of *past* actions (the ozone layer, the Earth's surface temperature, for example). How is the 'stock' of such assets to be measured? Valuation can assist but the prospect is fairly daunting. It becomes necessary to know not just the 'price' of global warming (the marginal damage done) but how that price will change over time. Similarly for tropical forests, wetlands, etc.

Economists, philosophers and ecologists are only just beginning to tackle the ways in which 'sustainability' could be measured (see the discussion in Chapter 2, and the box on page 51). Fairly clearly, many of the implications of sustainability, however defined, will be the same. Non-marketed assets must not be treated as if they have a zero price. Environmental impacts must be fully accounted for. The national income accounts must be modified. But whether it is enough to raise significantly the probability of securing sustainable development is not clear.

Modifying the discount rate

Environmentalists have traditionally been more concerned to see *actual* discount rates lowered. Four approaches to modifying discount rates may be considered. These are:

1 setting the discount rate equal to zero;
2 computing a consumer discount rate;
3 computing a producer discount rate; and
4 computing some weighted average of consumer and producer rates.

Zero discount rates
The argument for zero discount rates is essentially as follows. The point in time at which an individual exists cannot affect that individual's well-being. There has to be 'impartiality' about time. Well-being at one point of time cannot count more than well-being at another point of

time. This argument has a long tradition in utilitarianism, for example being clearly stated by Sidgwick. One defence of impartiality with respect to time is given by Rawls in terms of his 'original position' argument. An imaginary group of people coming together to determine an allocation of individuals to social groups and to time would not choose to favour one group or one time period over another since they would not know to which group or time period they themselves would be allocated. Thus there must be no discrimination between time periods if there is to be a 'just' allocation.

There are two sources of discounting. The first relates to the discounting of consumption streams and this would be justified by assumptions about diminishing marginal utility of income. The second relates to the discounting of utility itself. The latter is perhaps what is meant by true 'time preference', the former being due not to time but to differences in the levels of consumption. It can be shown that if time preference is zero and interest rates are positive (for the first reason) then any individual would rationally reduce consumption levels now to zero in order to make the marginal utility of such consumption infinite. Everything would be transferred to the future. Adopting a zero rate of discount for utility – which is what pure equality of treatment for generations would signify – would imply a policy of total current sacrifice. It would appear that zero rates may have implications contrary to the purpose advocated by those who want them.

Consumer discount rates
The standard formula for discounting future consumption is:

$$d_c = \sigma + \mu g$$

where d_c is the consumer discount rate, σ is the 'rate of pure time preference' (ie utility discounting), μ is the elasticity of the marginal utility of consumption function, and g is the growth rate of per capita consumption. If the utility function linking utility to consumption is logarithmic, then $\mu = 1$. If, further, pure time preference is rejected on ethical grounds, then $\sigma = 0$ and we have $d_c = g$. The discount rate becomes equal to the (expected) rate of growth of per capita consumption. Taking past growth rates as a guide to expected rates, the following box shows estimates of d_c for selected countries.

One result of this approach is that discount rates for the poorest countries become negative. Yet behaviour towards natural resource endowments in those countries is clearly inconsistent with this

ESTIMATING DISCOUNT RATES

Discount rates based on individuals' time preference can be estimated by using the equation given in the text. This requires an estimate of 'pure' time discounting, a measure of the elasticity of the marginal utility of income function, and an estimate of expected growth in real consumption per capita. Many experts ignore 'pure' time discounting and concentrate on the other components.

Table 10 *Estimates of selected national discount rates (% pa)*

Country	Growth of real private consumption (1)	Growth of population (2)	Discount rate (%) (1 – 2)
USA	3.3	1.0	+2.3
UK	2.8	0.2	+2.6
Japan	5.0	1.0	+4.0
Ethiopia	2.4	2.8	–0.4
Ghana	1.7	2.6	–0.9
Chile	0.8	1.7	–0.9
Thailand	5.8	2.5	+3.3

Note: assuming $\pi = 0$, $\mu = 1$

Source: Growth rates computed 1965–1988 from World Bank *World Development Report 1990* Oxford University Press, Oxford

outcome, ie resources are depleted *as if* personal discount rates are very high. Moreover, market lending rates are positive and high. The application of the income utility approach in these contexts may be questioned. It implies, for example, that as income doubles the household enjoys only half of the utility from the extra unit of income.

The box suggests that rates for industrialised and industrialising countries would appear to be in the range 2–4%. Estimates will, however, be conditioned by the past period used to make the calculation. Moreover, while the value of unity for μ is convenient some empirical work suggests values of around 1.5. The effect of $\mu = 1.5$ in the box is to raise the effective discount rates to 4% for the UK and USA, and over 6% in Thailand and Japan. The exclusion of σ from the estimates has also to be questioned. Little evidence exists about pure time preference rates in the industrialised world: a rate of 1.3% for the UK has been suggested, for example. Added to the rates in the box this would suggest a consumer discount rate in the UK inclusive of 'pure' time preference of about 4% for $\mu = 1$ and 5.3% for $\mu = 1.5$.

Producer discount rates

If capital markets were perfect, rates of return on capital would be equal to the rate d_c above. In practice, a number of distortions in the market place give rise to divergences between d_c and the producer rate of discount d_p. Corporation taxes, for example, mean that a company must earn r% if it is to pay its shareholders s% where:

$$r = s/(1-t)$$

where t is the corporation tax rate. Company taxation necessarily makes the producer borrowing rate higher than the rate at which consumers discount the future.

Many economists argue that r% is the 'correct' rate of discount because it measures the opportunity cost of using up $1 in public expenditure, ie it is the forgone rate of return on the marginal investment in the private sector. To find r one might take the weighted rate of return on equity and debt. The resulting long-run weighted average cost of capital to the private sector in the industrialised world would be perhaps 7% in real terms.

Clearly, if a discount rate of 7% is used, damages from distant environmental impacts such as global warming would appear insignificant in any benefit-cost comparison.

Synthetic discount rates

Any public expenditure on environmental controls would not simply be at the expense of private investment. It is more reasonable to suppose that it would be at the cost of some private investment and some consumption. If so, a 'synthetic' rate of the form:

$$s = w_p . d_p + w_c . d_c$$

would be appropriate. If it could be assumed that the weights for marginal investments are the same as the weights for existing expenditures, then the shares of consumption and investment in national income could be used. If a long-term consumption growth rate of 1.5% is used together with $\sigma = 0$ and $\mu = 1$, and $d_p = 7\%$, then a typical synthetic rate for an industrialised country with an 85% investment share in national income would become around 2.3%. It is difficult to argue that it is any lower than this.

CONCLUSIONS

There are two broad options for accommodating the distant nature of the effects of global warming and other environmental costs. The first requires that some intergenerational criterion of sustainability be imposed, leaving the 'conventional' discount rate unmodified as a means of allocating resources within a generation. The second involves seeking some quantitative adjustment to the conventional discount rate. The problem with the former adjustment is that, as yet, few specific rules for practical operation have emerged. Indeed, it may be that there is no requirement for special rules: each concerned individual simply argues for a 'fairer' allocation of resources to the future. The problem with the second approach is that it takes fairly heroic assumptions to make a *quantitative* adjustment that is other than arbitrary. The 'discounting problem' is not resolved either way in terms of real-world conclusions. If discount rates above 1–2% are used, an issue such as global warming is very unlikely to be seen as significant. Future generations would simply have to bear the cost. Rates of perhaps 2% *can* be justified if utility discounting is rejected as unethical – which seems valid given the whole idea is to account for intergenerational equity – if opportunity cost discounting is ignored, and if specific restrictions are placed on the nature of the income–utility function. Use of the opportunity cost rate *alone* does not appear justified, so that the appropriate range of estimates appears to be perhaps 2–5%.

Chapter 4

Valuation in practice

SETTING PRIORITIES

This chapter focuses on the issue of valuation mainly, but not exclusively, in the developing world. Chapter 1 indicated why it is important to engage in the activity of economic valuation. To the reasons given there we may now add another one. Increasingly, the world has come to recognise that the developing world has a limited capability for protecting its own environments, but an increasing need to do so since future development is unlikely to be sustainable without that protection. This recognition has been formalised in the recommendations of 'Agenda 21' at the Earth Summit conference at Rio de Janeiro in 1992, and in the conventions which govern the future control of greenhouse gas emissions and the protection of biological diversity. In short, there will have to be significant additional resource transfers from North to South. But the funds for such transfers are themselves limited, so that priorities need to be established. How can those funds best be used? The answer, again, has to lie in computing the 'rate of return' to such investments, and comparing rates of return across different kinds of investments, even if only in very broad brush terms. But investing in the environment produces the problem that the returns are not always marketed, as we have seen. Hence it is necessary to derive, as far as possible, economic values of benefit from such investments.

The economic valuation of environmental change and natural resources is reasonably well established in the developed world, but is a comparatively new activity for the developing world. Much valuation relies for its credibility on the existence of well-functioning property, goods and labour markets. In so far as these markets operate with extensive government intervention in the developing world, the scope for valuation appears to be more limited than in the developed world. This fact has not inhibited valuation studies in Eastern Europe where, perhaps surprisingly, valuations of the economic damage to the nation from pollution, especially air pollution, have been carried out on a fairly regular basis. But the problems of credibility of the estimates are high. Damage by acid rain to buildings, for example, has been estimated to be as high as $1.8 billion in Poland, or around 2.7% of GNP. If true, such losses would be massive and would justify significant expenditures on pollution control regardless of any impacts of air pollution on human health, crops and forests. But the methodologies used to arrive at such figures are primitive. Moreover, the prices used to value increased repair and rebuilding due to foreshortened building life are adminis-tered prices. The theory of valuation, however, requires that the prices used be market-clearing prices in the domestic market or border prices. As a result it is difficult to place limits of reliability on such estimates, making their policy relevance very doubtful.

Nor are valuation exercises in the developed world sufficiently advanced to give many insights into the setting of overall environmental priorities for the developing world. Few studies have compared benefits and costs for a single environmental medium (air, water etc) and fewer still have compared different media. As a result, it is difficult to say whether $1 in Europe, say, is better spent on controlling air pollution rather than water pollution. Even if this information was available, its implications for the developing world would not be readily transferable.

From the limited information available, the following speculative conclusions might be derived.

First, it seems reasonable to focus environmental policy on two broad targets: increasing net gains to GNP, and improving human health. Methods of raising GNP by environmental conservation and improve-ment need to be thought of in the broadest sense. Wildlife conservation may pay handsomely if it can be associated with tourist revenues. Conserving tropical forests may involve some 'development' sacrifices but could be rewarded if international resource transfers compensate for the losses. Attracting investment from the Global Environmental Facility would be an example. The focus on GNP ought to be contingent upon avoiding significant *irreversibilities*. That is, a GNP gain should not be sought at the cost of a major environmental cost that is irreversible and not recorded in conventional GNP.

Second, and focusing on GNP gains, investment in *soil conservation* and forms of *afforestation* would appear to have potentially high rates of return. Broad-brush calculations on soil conservation by the United Nations Food and Agriculture Organisation (FAO) suggest that unchecked erosion could cost some 19% of Asian, African and Central/South American crop output between 1975 and 2000. Some individual country studies of damage done produce very high estimates of damage. In Zimbabwe, for example, valuing nutrient losses from soil erosion in terms of the artificial fertilisers needed to replace them produced a staggering $1.5 billion estimate for 1985, one third of Zimbabwe's GNP. Clearly, the policy implication to be derived from this is not that GNP would rise by one-third in the absence of soil erosion. An anti-erosion policy would clearly cost significant resources itself. But the magnitudes are indicative of the kinds of gains to be had. Economic rates of return to soil conservation are also often high, although final judgement requires a far more substantial body of literature relating to the developing world rather than the well-buffered soils of some developed economies, and careful accounting for all costs and benefits.

In both cases of soil conservation and afforestation much of the return is likely to be in the form of *damage avoided* rather than visible net gains in the form of increased production. This presents a perception problem for farmers and others: investment to *maintain* economic activity tends to appear less attractive until the dramatic consequences of failing to prevent damage actually arise.

To some extent, the expectation that damage from soil erosion and biomass loss will be high may reflect the fact that, in a limited literature, these areas have been studied. The *economic* rate of return for improved water quality in the developing world is much under-researched. The number of work-days lost from waterborne diseases in Africa, Asia and Latin America, for example, may have totalled some 250 billion in the late 1970s. At just 50 cents per day this would amount to a staggering $125 billion lost output, perhaps 10% of gross world product for the relevant regions in the late 1970s. In the developing world high rates of return to water quality investment will almost certainly exceed rates of return to air pollution control. In the developed world, where drinking water quality largely precludes the presence of waterborne diseases, the balance may switch back towards air pollution control. In truth, however, valuation studies have not progressed far enough to underscore these conclusions.

FINDING WILLINGNESS TO PAY FOR CONSERVING ENVIRONMENTAL ASSETS

The notion of economic valuation rests on the concept of willingness to pay (WTP). The range of techniques available for eliciting willingness to pay is fairly wide (see Appendix II). Their application in the developing world is very recent. Some examples reveal the usefulness of investigating the applicability of WTP techniques.

Valuing protected areas

Protecting wilderness areas tends to be a low national priority in many developing countries. This is especially true where protected land competes with the demand for land for agricultural extensification, and where domestic values for land are low relative to the 'global' value afforded it by residents of other countries. Notable examples of the former include many of the national parks in Africa, and the latter would be typified by tropical forests, unique wetlands, coral reefs and mangrove swamps which tend to be rich in biological diversity.

Some sense of economic value can be obtained by looking at the

---

IMPLICIT WILLINGNESS TO PAY FOR ENVIRONMENTAL ASSETS IN INTERNATIONAL TRANSFERS

Debt-for-nature swaps

Numerous debt-for-nature swaps have been agreed. Table II below sets out the available information and computes the implicit prices. It is not possible to be precise with respect to the implicit prices since the swaps tend to cover not just protected areas but education and training as well. Moreover, each hectare of land does not secure the same degree of 'protection' and the same area may be covered by different swaps. We have also arbitrarily chosen a 10 year horizon in order to compute present values whereas the swaps in practice have variable levels of annual commitment.

Ignoring the outlier (Monteverde Cloud Forest, Costa Rica) the range of implicit values is from around 1 cent/ha to just over 4 dollars/ha. Ruitenbeek (1992) secures a range of some 18 cents to $11/ha (ignoring Monteverde) but has several different areas for some of the swaps and he also computes a present value of outlays for the swaps. But either range is very small compared to the opportunity costs of protected land, although if these implicit prices mean anything they are capturing only part of the rich world's existence values for these assets. That is, the values reflect only part of the total economic value.

Finding a benchmark from such an analysis is hazardous but something of the order of $5/ha seems appropriate.

Table 11 *Implicit willingness to pay in debt-for-nature swaps*

Country	Date	Payment (1990$)	Area (m ha PV)	WTP/ha (1990$)	Notes
Bolivia	8/87	112,000	12.00	0.01	1
Ecuador	12/87	354,000	} 22.00	0.06	2
	4/89	1,068,750			
Costa Rica:					
	2/88	918,000	1.15	0.80	3
	7/88	5,000,000			
4 parks	1/89	784,000			
	4/89	3,500,000	0.81	4.32	4
La Amistad	3/90	1,953,473	1.40	1.40	5
Monteverde	1/91	360,000	0.014	25.70	6
Dominican Rep.	3/90	116,400			
Guatemala	10/91	75,000			
Jamaica	11/91	300,000			
Philippines	1/89	200,000	} 9.86	0.06	7
	8/90	438,750			
	2/92	5,000,000			
Madagascar	7/89	950,000	} 0.47	2.95	8
	8/90	445,891			
	1/91	59,377			9
Mexico	2/91	180,000			
Nigeria	7/91	64,788			
Zambia	8/89	454,000			10
Poland	1/90	11,500	unrelated to area purchase		
Nigeria	1989	1,060,000	1.84	0.58	11

Notes
A discount rate of 6% is used, together with a time horizon of 10 years. The sum of discount factors for 10 years is then 7.36.
  1. The Beni 'park' is 334,000 acres and the surrounding buffer zones are some 3.7 million acres, making 1.63 million *hectares* in all (1 hectare = 2.47 acres). 1.63 × 7.36 = 12 million hectares in present value terms.
  2. Covers 6 areas: Cayembe Coca Reserve at 403,000 ha; Cotacachi-Cayapas at 204,000 ha; Sangay National Park at 370,000 ha; Podocarpus National Park at 146,280 ha; Cuyabeno Wildlife Reserve at 254,760 ha; Yasuni National Park –

no area stated; Galapagos National Park at 691,2000 ha; Pasochoa near Quito at 800 ha. The total without Yasuni is therefore 2.07 mha. Inspection of maps suggests that Yasuni is about three times the area of Sangay, say 1 mha. This would make the grand total some 3 mha. The PV of this over 10 years is then 22 mha. This is more than twice the comparable figure quoted in Ruitenbeek (1992).

3. Covers Corvocado at 41,788 ha; Guanacaste at 110,000 ha; Monteverde Cloud Forest at 3,600 ha, to give 156,600 ha in all, or a present value of land area of 1.15 m ha. Initially, $5.4 million at face value, purchased for $912,000, revalued here to 1990 prices.

4. Guanacaste at 110,000 ha, to give a PV of 0.81 mha.

5. La Amistad at 190,000 ha, to give a PV of 1.4 mha.

6. Monteverde Cloud Forest at 2023 ha × 7.36 = 14,900 ha.

7. Area 'protected' is 5753 ha of St Paul Subterranean River National Park, and 1.33 m ha of El Nido National Marine Park. This gives a PV of land of 9.86 m.ha.

8. Focus on Adringitra and Marojejy reserves at 31,160 ha and 60,150 ha respectively. This gives a PV of 474,000 ha.

9. Covers four reserve areas: Zahamena, Midongy-Sud, Manongarivo and Namoroko.

10. Covers Kafue Flats and Bangweulu wetlands.

11. Oban park, protecting 250,000 ha or 1.84 m ha in PV terms. See Ruitenbeek (1992).

Source: Ruitenbeek (1992) and Pearce et al (1992c)

implied valuations in existing international conservation schemes. This is particularly relevant to *debt-for-nature* swaps where secondary debt is bought by a conservationist concern and then traded with the host government for a domestic currency liability and a conservation package. The box above shows the results of translating the sums paid in a number of debt-for-nature swaps into 'per hectare' values. The figures shown appear to be very small, perhaps a few dollars per hectare of land. It has to be remembered that debt-for-nature swaps do not 'purchase' land as such but secure rights to conserve the land, or operate on it in a sustainable manner. As such, the prices shown are not market-clearing prices. Also important is the fact that the sums paid understate true willingness to pay. The swaps are managed by a few conservation bodies and governments. The resulting deals do not necessarily reflect what would happen if wider populations were to engage in the process of expressing their willingness to pay. Nonetheless, debt-for-nature swaps are (so far) the only way in which we have secured estimates of what might be existence value. Actually carrying out a contingent valuation exercise of the North's willingness to pay for environmental assets in the South would be another way of achieving this goal, and such exercises are planned.

More explicit valuations of protected areas are comparatively few in developing countries. An exercise in Khao Yai national park near Bangkok in Thailand suggested recreational benefits of some 10–25 million baht per year, and possible 'existence' benefits of more than 120 million baht per year. These might be compared to management costs and forgone farm income of about 30 million baht. Provided existence values can be 'captured', eg through raising entrance charges to the park, the analysis suggests a high return to conservation. Similar analysis of a wildlife sanctuary in Khao Sol Dao, Thailand, where tourism is not encouraged, produced a series of 'indeterminate' values which, in principle, could be estimated with further data and resources.

Valuing the ecological functions of wetlands

The world's wetlands are under threat from agricultural, residential and industrial development, and from pollution. Wetlands comprise areas of marsh, fens, mangroves, and other wet areas usually, but not always, at the interface between aquatic and terrestrial environments. They account for some 6% of the global land area. They are especially fragile ecosystems because they are 'open' and are fed by river systems which are themselves subject to pollution and man-made changes in flow. Because their economic functions have been so poorly understood, they also tend to be regarded as being relatively unimportant. But there is now a wider appreciation that wetlands are *multifunctional* and that many of the unpriced functions are economically important (see Table 12).

Table 13 shows some estimates of the economic values of wetlands. By themselves they are of little interest, apart from showing that wetlands *do* have economic value and the value is not negligible. Of more relevance is the relationship between these economic values and the values of the alternative use of the wetlands. It is often assumed that water feeding a wetland is not serving a useful function when in fact, as Table 13 shows, natural wetlands serve a number of direct economic functions such as supporting agriculture and fisheries. Proposals to drain wetlands by diverting water resources to, say, irrigation of adjacent areas or to reclaim the wetland soils should therefore be debited with the forgone benefits of the natural system. In the case of the Hadeja-Jama'are floodplains of northern Nigeria it has been

Table 12 *The ecological functions of wetlands*

Wetland Types	Wetland Functions/Services
a) Inland freshwater marshes	1) (a, b, e, f, g) Nutrient cycling and storage: resulting in potential water quality improvement
b) Inland saline marshes	2) (a, c, e, f, g) Potential aquifer or groundwater storage and recharge function
c) Bogs	3) (all except perhaps d) Provision of a delay mechanism for the release of flood waters; storm protection from tidal surges and winds
d) Tundra	4) (a, b, g, h, i, j) Shoreline anchoring (coastal and riverine) providing a buffer against erosion
e) Shrub swamp	5) (all) Ameliorating influences on local microclimates and a possible biospherical stabilisation role, carbon sinks etc
f) Wooded swamp	6) (all to varying degrees) Food web support (local and extended)
g) Wet meadows, bottomlands and other riparian habitats	7) (all to varying degrees) commercial outputs: fish, furs, timber, wildfowl, peat fuel, reed, low-intensity grazing
h) Coastal salt marshes	8) (all to varying degrees) Recreational opportunities
i) Mangrove swamps	9) (all to varying degrees) Other, eg wildlife habitats, landscape assets; non-use values likely to be very significant for unique high-rank order wetlands
j) Tidal freshwater marshes	

Source: Turner, K and Jones, T (1991) *Wetlands: Market and Intervention Failures – Four Case Studies* Earthscan, London

possible to show that even a *partial* valuation of natural functions reveals the superiority of the wetland as an agricultural, fishery and fuelwood supply system compared to the alternative of damming feeder rivers. A useful way of presenting such findings is in terms of the net economic value per cubic metre of water supplied to the wetland system. In the Hadeja-Jama're case the resulting comparison showed

Table 13 *Economic values for wetlands functions*

Area	Source of value	Valuation ($ per acre)
Louisiana (1)	Commercial fishery	400
	Fur Trapping	190
	Recreation	57
	Storm protection	2400
	Total	3047
Louisiana (2)	Recreation	103
Charles River, Mass (3)	Recreation	3400
	Water supply	80000
Hadejia-Jama'are Floodplain, Nigeria (4)	Agriculture	41
	Fishing	15
	Fuelwood	7
	Total	63
Mangrove: Trinidad (5)	Mainly fisheries	15000
Fiji (5)		11000
Puerto Rico (5)		13000

Notes and sources
All reported valuations have been converted to 1990 prices and to 8% discount rates.
1. Costanza, R, Farber, S and Maxwell, J (1989) 'Valuation and Management of Wetland Ecosystems' *Ecological Economics*, vol 1, no 4, December, pp 335–362
2. Bergstrom, J, Stoll, J, Titre, J and Wright, V (1990) 'Economic Value of Wetlands-Based Recreation' *Ecological Economics*, vol 2, no 2, June, pp 129–148
3. Thibodeau, F and Ostro, B (1981) 'An Economic Analysis of Wetland Protection' *Journal of Environmental Management* vol 12, no 1, January
4. Barbier, E, Adams, W and Kimmage, K (1991) *Economic valuation of Wetland Benefits: the Hadejia-Jama'are Floodplain, Nigeria* London Environmental Economics Centre, Paper 91–02, London
5. *Handbook for Mangrove Area Management*, Section IV.

net benefits of $45 per 1000m³ of water flow for the natural system, but only 4 *cents* per 1000m³ for an existing diversion of water through the building of a dam. A similar analysis of Ichkeul National Park in Tunisia, also threatened by dams, showed fishery and grazing benefits of $134 per 1000m³ of water compared to *negative* returns for the diversionary use (see Thomas et al, 1990). It cannot always be assumed that there is profit in nature, nor that, when there is, it will exceed man-made alternatives, but the evidence is sufficient to show that the alternative mistake of assuming that natural systems have low economic value is a serious one.

Valuing preferences for peace and quiet

Noise nuisance afflicts all societies in the workplace and in the open where the main causes are traffic noise and, in the richer world, aircraft noise. Attempts to value people's preferences for peace and quiet have centred on the use of the *hedonic price approach* (see Appendix II) whereby an analysis is made of the determinants of house prices. A residential property price will vary with the characteristics of the property – its location, size, neighbourhood, nearness to the business district and shopping, and so on. In this way the house is seen more as a 'bundle of attributes' rather than bricks and mortar. By statistically analysing the prices of different properties according to their attributes it is possible to separate out the factors influencing prices, factors that will include the local noise level. Table 14 shows the results of various studies of the relationship between noise levels and house prices. They are presented in terms of a 'price elasticity', ie for each unit change in the noise level, measured in standard noise units, the percentage change in property price is shown. For aircraft noise the estimates suggest that for every unit change in NEF (noise exposure forecast) property prices might change by around 1%, and for every unit change in NNI (noise and number index) the change is around 0.5%. For traffic noise, measured in Leq (equivalent continuous sound level), a one unit change again produces property price depreciation of 0.5–1.0%. Clearly, using property price changes to measure preferences for reducing noise nuisance does not encompass all the benefits of noise reduction. High and continuous levels of noise are probably associated with health impairment through stress, for example. It is unlikely that individuals will be sufficiently aware of health risks to 'capture' their value in the form of house location choice. None the less, the hedonic property price

Table 14 *The economic value of reducing noise nuisance*

Study	Impact of 1 Unit Change in	
	NEF	NNI
AIRCRAFT NOISE		
USA		
Los Angeles		0.8
Englewood		0.8
New York	1.6–2.0	
Minneapolis	0.6	
San Francisco	0.5	
Boston	0.8	
Washington DC	1.0	
Dallas	0.6–0.8	
Rochester	0.6–0.7	
Canada		
Toronto		0.2–0.6
Edmonton	0.1–1.6	
UK		
Heathrow		0.2–0.3
Manchester		0.0
Australia		
Sydney	0.0–0.4	
Switzerland		
Basel		0.2
Netherlands		
Amsterdam		0.3–0.5
Norway		
Bode	1.0 (per dB)	
Average:	0.6–1.3	0.2–0.5
TRAFFIC NOISE	Leq	
USA		
N Virginia	0.1	
Tidewater	0.1	
N Springfield	0.2–0.5	
Towson	0.5	
Washington DC	0.9	
Kingsgate	0.5	
North King County	0.3	

Spokane	0.1
Chicago	0.7
Canada	
Toronto	1.0
Switzerland	
Basel	1.3
Norway	
Oslo	0.8
AVERAGE	0.5

Sources: OECD (1989) *Environmental Policy Benefits: Monetary Valuation* OECD, Paris; Nelson, J (1980) 'Airports and Property Values: a Survey of Recent Evidence' *Journal of Transport Economics and Policy*, XIV, pp 37–52; Nelson, J (1982) 'Highway Noise and Property Values: a Survey of Recent Evidence' *Journal of Transport Economics and Policy*, XVI, pp 117–130; Navrud, S (1991) 'Norway' in Barde, JPh and Pearce, D W, *Valuing the Environment* Earthscan, London

approach offers a reasonable approach to the valuation of the dominant benefit of noise reduction – reduced irritation and nuisance.

Valuing preferences for unique habitat

The 'existence' value component of total economic value can be important, particularly where the object of valuation is unique (as with the Grand Canyon or a cultural building) or, if not unique, the subject of extensive familiarity to people some distance from the asset. The Kakadu Conservation Zone in northern Australia is a 50km square zone surrounded by the 20,000km square Kakadu National Park. The Park is visited by over 200,000 people every year and has outstanding scenery, wildlife, wetlands and Aboriginal archaeological sites. Mining operations threatened to disrupt the Conservation Zone. Australia's Resource Assessment Commission therefore determined to elicit economic values for the Zone in order to compare them to the benefits of mining development. The approach used was *contingent valuation* (see Appendix 2) whereby respondents are asked to complete a questionnaire which includes questions about willingness to pay to conserve the area. The resulting 'market' is hypothetical and hence the problem with this method is to test for 'hypothetical bias', ie the extent to which answers given to hypothetical questions would be borne out if there was a 'real' market in conservation. Part of this bias-minimisation process involves asking 'discrete choice' questions in which respondents answer yes or no to a specified question about willingness to pay, rather than answering questions about what their willingness to pay is.

The Kakadu valuation produced the following results:

Type of Mining Impact	Valuation: $A/year for 10 years	
	National sample	*Northern Territory sample*
Major	124–143	7–35
Minor	53–80	14–33

with the analysts showing a preference for the lower end of the range, so that valuations are some $A 50–120 per year for the national sample, according to whether the mining development would have a minor or major impact, and $7–14 for the minor impact. Extrapolated to the whole Australian population the total willingness to pay to conserve the area against mining ranges from $650 million to $1750 million, greatly in excess of the net benefits from mining (see Imber et al, 1991). Contingent valuation is controversial partly because of its use of 'hypothetical questions', but also because it is the only valuation technique capable of capturing the option and existence value components of total economic value. No attempt was made in the Kakadu study to separate out the component parts of value, but it is clear that much of the stated willingness to pay was made on behalf of people who were very unlikely to visit the area. How far the valuations recorded would be validated if there was a real market in conservation of the Kakadu Conservation Zone is unknown. There are some reasons for supposing that so-called 'framing bias' arises in highly targeted valuation studies of this kind: individuals state a willingness to pay for a single purpose without reference to the many alternative uses of the money they say they are willing to pay. Some commentators feel that framing bias is particularly relevant when it comes to valuing endangered species.

Valuing preferences for the conservation of endangered species

Contingent valuation techniques currently provide the only available technique for eliciting preference valuations for environmental assets that have no related market. Endangered species provide one such example. The problem with the contingent valuation method (CVM) is that because the market is created experimentally – through the use of interviews and questionnaires – there is no obvious way to *validate* the estimated willingness to pay (WTP) for conservation. A great deal of the CVM literature is therefore concerned with procedures for validation (see Appendix II). Broadly speaking, validation tests include (a) checking the CVM results against other valuation techniques (usually the travel cost method – see Appendix II), (b) checking for biases in responses to the questionnaire, and (c) checking, where possible, against actual market-revealed willingness to pay.

One virtue of the CVM approach is that it alone can capture 'existence' and 'option' values. All other valuation techniques focus on *use* values. Table 15 shows the results of CVM studies for endangered or rare species, and highly valued ecosystems. The various estimates have been converted to per person WTP in 1990 prices. The data are interesting because of their broad consistency. Valuations of preferences for species conservation, for example, cluster around $9 if the relatively high value for humpback whales is excluded, and $13 if they are included. The range is $1–18 excluding humpback whales and $1–48 including humpback whales (see note in Table 15). For prized habitat the range is $9–107 per person per year. While a great deal more work is needed in this area, the results are suggestive in that (a) they are not large proportions of respondent income, and (b) habitat appears more highly valued than species which, given the role that habitat conservation would play in species conservation, is the difference one would expect: a wider array of benefits is being secured through conservation of habitat than through targeting species.

One problem area is clearly framing bias. The sum of the species valuations in the USA, for example, is much higher than average personal contributions to conservation societies, although the latter may reflect 'free rider' phenomena (many who value the environment do not pay because others pay). The international comparison of per capita values is also problematic. There are no particular reasons to suppose that 'unit values' of this kind would be the same between countries or even between different regions of the same country. But where there are reasons to suppose that environmental awareness is on approximately the same scale – which is testable through opinion polls – then, allowing for variations in income, one might expect similar

Table 15 *Preference valuations for endangered species and prized habitats*

Country	Species or habitat	Valuation (1990 US$/year/person)
Norway	brown bear, wolf and wolverine	15.0
USA	bald eagle	12.4
	emerald shiner	4.5
	grizzly bear	18.5
	bighorn sheep	8.6
	whooping crane	1.2
	blue whale	9.3
	bottlenose dolphin	7.0
	California sea otter	8.1
	northern elephant seal	8.1
	humpback whales[1]	40–48 (without information)
		49–64 (with information)
USA	Grand Canyon (visibility)	27.0
	Colorado wilderness	9.3–21.2
Australia		
	Nadgee Nature Reserve, NSW	28.1
	Kakadu Conservation Zone, NT[2]	40.0 (minor damage)
		93.0 (major damage)
UK	nature reserves[3]	40.0 ('experts' only)
Norway	conservation of rivers against hydroelectric development	59.0–107.0

Notes: (1) respondents divided into two groups one of which was given video information; (2) two scenarios of mining development damage were given to respondents; (3) survey of informed individuals only

Sources
Norway: Dahle, L et al (1987) 'Attitudes Towards and Willingness to pay For Brown Bear, Wolverine and Wolf in Norway' Department of Forest Economics, Agricultural University of Norway, Report 5 (in Norwegian); Hervik, A et al (1986) 'Implicit Costs and Willingness to Pay for Development of Water Resources' in A Carlsen (ed) *Proceedings of UNESCO Symposium on Decision Making in Water Resources Planning* May, Oslo
USA: Boyle, K and Bishop, R (1985) 'The Total Value of Wildlife Resources: Conceptual and Empirical Issues' Paper presented to Association of Environmental and Resource Economists, Boulder, May; Brookshire, D et al (1983) 'Estimating Option Prices and Existence Values for Wildlife Resources' *Land Economics* 59; Stoll, R and Johnson, L (1984) 'Concepts of Value, Non-market Valuation, and the Case of the Whooping Crane',

Department of Agricultural Economics, Texas A&M University; Hageman, R (1985) 'Valuing Marine Mammal Populations: Benefit Valuations in a Multi-Species Ecosystem' National Marine Fisheries Service, Southwest Fisheries Center, Report LJ-85-22, La Jolla, California; Samples, K et al (1986) 'Information Disclosure and Endangered Species Valuation' *Land Economics*, vol 62, no 3; Schulze, W et al (1983) 'Economic Benefits of Preserving Visibility in the National Parklands of the Southwest' *Natural Resources Journal* 23; Walsh, R et al (1984) 'Valuing Option, Existence and Bequest Demands for Wilderness' *Land Economics*, vol 60, no 1
Australia: Imber, D et al (1991) *A Contingent Valuation Survey of the Kakadu Conservation Zone* Resource Assessment Commission, Research Paper No 3, Canberra, February; Bennett, J (1982) 'Using Direct Questioning to Value Existence Benefits of Preserved Natural Areas' School of Business Studies, Darling Downs Institute of Education, Toowoomba
United Kingdom: Willis, K and Benson, J (1988) 'Valuation of Wildlife: A Case Study on the Upper Teesdale Site of Special Scientific Interest and Comparison of Methods in Environmental Economics' in R K Turner (ed) *Sustainable Environmental Management* Belhaven Press, London

valuations. As yet little work has been done to test this 'transferability' of values.

Willingness to pay for rural water supplies

Valuation techniques have also been applied to the more immediate human environment – notably water supply and sanitation. Traditionally, water supply investments have been evaluated by rules of thumb related to assumed willingness to pay for basic services. Since the service is usually supplied to the poor, the assumption has been that only the most basic provision – public taps and hand pumps – is warranted. No-one is willing to pay for better, more elaborate services. This 'basic needs' philosophy would be satisfactory if the resulting public supplies were reliable. But perhaps one in four public supply systems are not working at any one point of time, while use rates of those that do work are low – only one-third of people connected to public supply systems in Côte d'Ivoire and Kenya actually use them. Yet the benefits of such systems in terms of public health and time saving are clearly substantial. Households' true willingness to pay is therefore worth estimating.

In the absence of real markets in which price varies, the challenge is to find the underlying demand for the service. In terms of *time saving* one approach is to observe how people choose between alternative sources of supply. In Ukundu, Kenya villagers could choose between water from vendors who visit the house, water sold at 'kiosks' in the village, and water from the well (see Mu et al, 1989). In terms of *collection time*, relative to use of the well, house delivery saves the most collection time and collecting from wells the least amount of time. In terms of *expenditure*, household vending costs the most, then kiosk water, with well water being the cheapest. By looking at actual choices, the trade-off between money and time can be determined. Time saving is one of the benefits of water supply improvement. In this case, if water quality is invariant between sources, time savings will generally define total benefits. The Ukundu study found that users of vendors and kiosks were revealing high WTP for time savings, of the order of 8% of incomes.

A study in Brazil used the *contingent valuation approach* (see Appendix II) which essentially involves asking people either directly what they are willing to pay, or less directly what their choice would be if they were faced with certain prices for the service in question (see Briscoe et al, 1990). In the Brazilian study, the question took the form 'If you are required to pay X, would you connect to the new supply or use an alternative supply?'. Three different areas were surveyed, some with improved services available, to which households might or might not be connected, and some without. In the 'without' cases some had services planned with an announced tariff, others expected a service but did not know of what kind or what the tariff would be. From the survey the probabilities of being connected were estimated, and these were found to behave as predicted. The higher the price and the greater the distance to the source, the less likely was connection. WTP estimates were also obtained from the questionnaires. The results provide not just an estimate of the average WTP, but also indicate how households would respond to higher prices, an important consideration if revenue-raising is a concern. Maximum WTP for a yard tap was around 2.5 times the prevailing tariff and some 2.3% of family income. Some 'strategic bias' – deliberate under-reporting of WTP – was probably present (see Appendix II) so that true WTP was probably higher than this. Equity considerations could be taken care of by providing relatively highly priced services to the better off and using revenues to cross-subsidise the needs of the poor for free public taps.

The benefits of improved sanitation

Sanitation needs in developing countries will become a greater and greater burden on public revenues as urban populations grow rapidly.

Less than 300 million people lived in developing country urban areas in 1950. Today the figure is over 1300 million. By 2000 it will be 1.9 billion. By the year 2000 there will be 200 cities with populations over 1 million people, of which 150 will be in developing countries. The cost of the necessary infrastructure for this urban development is enormous. As with water supply generally, sanitation systems tend to be primitive for the poor and subsidised systems of the less primitive schemes tend to benefit the middle and upper income classes. And as with water, willingness to pay is generally *assumed* rather than estimated. Charges above 3% of household incomes are thought not to be affordable.

In Kumasi, Ghana, WTP was estimated through a contingent valuation approach. The options were water closets with a piped sewerage system and ventilated pit latrines ('KVIPs'). The latter represent a far cheaper option for sanitation than connecting sewers and installing water closets. Households varied according to the systems already in place. Some had water connections and could therefore be asked their WTP for a water closet and a KVIP. Households with water closets could be asked how much they would be willing to pay for a connection to the sewer, and so on. KVIPs can operate without water connections. The results showed that households without water closets were willing to pay roughly the same sum for a WC or a KVIP. In terms of WTP for KVIPs, households with bucket latrines bid the lowest price; those using public latrines bid significantly higher prices (around 30–35% more), reflecting the inconvenience and lack of privacy of the public systems. Overall mean bids of around $1.5 per month compare to average existing expenditures of about $0.5 per month. Comparing WTP with the costs of provision of KVIPs and WCs, WTP was found to be *less* than costs of supply. Given that sanitation systems yield extensive external benefits in the form of public health, a subsidy would probably be justified (the benefits of improved health were not estimated). The study showed that the required subsidy for a WC system for Kumasi would amount to some $60 million. The required overall subsidy for the KVIP system would amount to some $4 million (see Whittington et al, 1991).

Valuing the benefits of fuelwood planting

In the developing world wood still accounts for the major part of energy consumption. Planting trees for fuelwood is thus an inherently valuable activity, but how valuable? Since much fuelwood is collected rather than purchased in the marketplace there are no market prices at which to value the commodity. Moreover, growing trees yield benefits besides fuelwood. Trees provide poles for building, leaves for fodder, protection for crops, and so on. Economic valuation techniques are therefore essential if the benefits of investing in tree growing are to be demonstrated. Typical approaches to valuing *fuelwood* benefits involve estimating what other source of energy would be used if increased fuelwood is not available. This might involve supplies of kerosene, coal if available, and cow dung. If it is kerosene or coal then market prices are available. Cow dung may also be marketed but this will typically be the case where fuelwood is also marketed, ie in conditions of considerable scarcity, so that fuelwood market prices are then available. The value of cow dung can be estimated by looking at the responsiveness of crops to cow dung as a fertiliser and soil conditioner. The market value of the crops then provides the relevant link to the world of market values. Care has to be taken that the predicted substitution is credible. In Korea some fuelwood investments have been justified on the basis that the alternative fuel would be coal. In the event, the fuelwood did not displace coal. Rather, coal displaced fuelwood in rural areas. As with all project appraisal, predicting tastes and preferences can be hazardous.

The valuation of fuelwood by comparison with cow dung can be estimated as follows. First, find the energy content of fuelwood and dung. Second, estimate the weight of fuelwood in a cubic metre. Third, compute the 'dung equivalent' of 1 cubic metre of fuelwood by multiplying the weight by the ratio of the energy values of fuelwood and dung. Fourth, estimate the amount of manure that a given amount of dung produces, so that the cubic metre of fuelwood can now be expressed in 'manure equivalent'. Fifth, estimate the crop yield response to this amount of manure and the monetary value of this yield increase. Sixth, normalise the value of the yield increase per cubic metre of fuelwood: this is then the economic value, or shadow price, of the fuelwood.

The steps in this process are not complex but the validity of the final result is crucially dependent upon the crop yield response estimates. As with so much economic valuation it is not the *economic* stages in the process that give rise to the problem, but the underlying 'production function', ie the links between the environmental variable and the economic variable. Similar approaches to the 'dung-equivalent' method have been used in a number of economic appraisals and in estimating soil erosion damage. Sometimes the costs and benefits are estimated in terms of the *chemical* equivalents. For example, instead of the 'manure' equivalent, it is possible to estimate the amount of commercial fertiliser that would have to be used to compensate for cow dung diverted from use as a manure to use as a fuel because of fuelwood scarcity. This was the approach used in a World Bank study of afforestation in Ethiopia (see Newcombe, 1989). Such approaches do not capture all the benefits of fuelwood since the chemical nutrient status of dung is only part of its value as a manure. None the less, the procedure reveals that environmental costs and benefits invariably do have an analogue somewhere in the private market system. The challenge for valuation is to make that link and translate the market values back to the environmental asset.

Fuelwood investment yields other benefits too. The closer proximity of the wood to the point of use means that valuable labour time is saved. Past studies have typically valued the saved time at the ruling wage rate if there is no surplus labour, and at the minimum wage where there is surplus labour. Strictly, neither approach is correct in terms of the criterion of willingness to pay. Rather the requirement is for some valuation based on actual choices, as with the Ukundu study above. Trees also provide leaf fodder for animals and this is often included in project evaluations. Again, if fodder is not actually marketed, a 'production function' link can be made to marketed outputs by estimating the effects of increased fodder on livestock weight and hence the market value of livestock. Care has to be taken to apply the 'with' and 'without' principle. If trees are grown especially for fodder, then the loss of output from the existing use of the land has to be deducted. Grass yields forgone, for example, would be deducted from tree fodder yields.

Trees as inhibitors of 'desertification' may also be important, where desertification needs to be construed as general land degradation rather than the more popular and unwarranted concept of 'spreading deserts'. The idea is that any tree planting tends to reduce pressure on naturally forested land. One approach to value the gains is to estimate the fuelwood yield from plantations (X) and compare it to yields from the natural forest areas (Y). Each hectare of plantation can then be said to 'save' X/Y hectares of natural forest land. Monetising the 'avoided damage' might then take place by projecting the rate of soil erosion on the natural forest land so that, after some threshold year, all crop and livestock production from that land would be lost. By calculating the present value of lost output, a surrogate value for the benefits of planting trees is obtained.

The fuelwood valuation issue reveals several important lessons. First, valuation *is* possible. Second, the underlying ecological interlinkages are the vital element in the valuation process. The highest rewards are likely to be obtained from expanding our knowledge of these inter-dependencies. Third, it is essential to look at *all* potential benefits. In the event some may turn out not to be important, but the fodder and anti-desertification examples show that some of the 'incidental' benefits could be significant.

Valuing the benefits of biological diversity

Probably the greatest challenge to economic valuers is to derive some values for people's preferences for biological diversity. 'Biodiversity' is frequently used as a shorthand for both the *quantity* and the *range* of species, and equally frequently as a catch-all phrase for *wildlife* and *habitat*. Strictly, biodiversity refers to all species of plants, animals and micro-organisms and the ecosystems and ecological processes of which they are parts. Increasingly, economists are turning their attention to the issues of valuing preferences for biodiversity. The example of endangered species has already been given. This section extends the examples.

The African elephant

Kenya is visited by about 250,000 foreign adult tourists every year. The 'safari' is the main focus of this tourism, with around $200 million per year actually being spent in Kenya and perhaps twice that on the visits overall (much of the income accrues to the industry in the tourist's country of origin). Until a recent ban on the ivory trade, the Kenyan elephant was disappearing very rapidly. From 65,000 elephants in 1981, there were probably only 16,000 by the end of the 1980s. An analysis of expenditures by tourists (the *travel cost approach* – see Appendix II) and a *contingent valuation* approach suggested that tourists would be willing to pay an extra $25 million pa to ensure that they saw elephants during their stay. Points of comparison are that (a) this represents at least a 10% increase in actual expenditures, and (b) it is substantially higher than even the peak value of (largely illegal) ivory exports in 1979 at $3 million, and higher still than the estimated 1988 value of only $17,000 (see Brown and Hall, 1989). In policy terms it suggests that countries with significant wildlife resources and a demand by tourists to see them could extract some of the 'rent' that tourists obtain.

Birds

Few studies exist of the economic significance of birds. One Canadian study looked at the direct benefits from recreational and other activities associated with birds (Jacquemot and Filion, 1987). Over 100,000 people were surveyed to see their actual participation in bird-related activities and to ask their willingness to pay to participate. Expenditures by participants amounted to C$ 1.9 billion (1986 C$) and incremental benefits (the excess of WTP over actual costs) were some C$ 350 million. For all wildlife (birds and mammals) the total net benefit was C$780 million pa. Birds thus accounted for around 45% of all wildlife-related activity net benefits. Of the expenditures on bird-related activity – which results in direct income and employment to others – half was accounted for by *non-consumptive* activities (ie birdwatching). Bird-related expenditure accounted for some C$2.4 billion of Canadian GDP, and for C$ 870 million of government revenues. Protection of a single species often results in significant gains from recreational viewing. Canada's 'capistrano' (the Pembroke swallow) was protected in 1983. The mass flocking of these birds produces a spectacle much appreciated by recreationists. Estimated net benefits, based on the *travel cost approach* (Appendix II) were some C$ 0.5 million pa (see Clark, 1987).

Ecotourism

The travel cost method has been applied to the valuation that visitors place on the Monteverde Cloud Forest Biological Reserve in Costa Rica (Tobias and Mendelsohn, 1991). The reserve is mainly virgin rainforest with difficult access, but with a growing tourist demand. Domestic visitors were sampled to find their area of origin, and the distances they had travelled were calculated. Distance was converted to currency using an average cost per kilometre of US$ 0.15 per kilometre. A demand function was then estimated linking visits to cost of travel (the price), population density and a measure of literacy in each of the areas of origin. The expected links were (a) the higher the cost the lower the visit rate, (b) the higher the population density the higher the visit rate (low density populations would be more likely to have their own forest areas to visit), (c) the higher the literacy (and hence the higher is permanent income) the higher will be the visit rate. This is indeed what was found. Estimated visits were found to correspond to actual visits.

From the demand function it was possible to estimate the 'consumer surplus', the excess of willingness-to-pay over the actual cost of travel. The sum of these valuations expressed as a present value was US$ 2.4–2.9 million for this one site, or around $35 per visit, or some $100,000 per year. This figure *excludes* foreign visitors who outnumbered domestic visitors by four to one in 1988. Assuming a similar per capita valuation, this would mean present values of $2.5–10 million, or some $1250 per hectare. New land can be bought for $30–100 per hectare, suggesting that expanding the reserve to allow for more recreation would be a worthwhile investment.

The economic value of plant-based pharmaceuticals

No-one is sure just how many species there are. A probable number for *higher plant* species, which are widely used as bases for pharmaceutical drugs, is some 500,000, counting known and unknown species. Rates of extinction are positive but again unknown. Perhaps 10% or more of these species will be extinct by the end of the century. Of all the higher plant species, 65–75% are indigenous to tropical moist forests. Hence loss of rainforest means losing *potential* sources of future pharmaceuticals. Actual, existing, sources are likely to be protected through replication and synthesising of materials. What is the economic value of these plants? Valuation to date has been fairly speculative but illustrative of the orders of magnitude involved. Valuation can be approached by looking at:

1   the actual market value of the plants when traded;
2   the market value of the drugs of which they are the source material; and
3   the value of the drugs in terms of their life-saving properties, and using a value of a 'statistical life'.

If we do not take into account the prevailing institutional capability to capture the values in discoveries as implied in 2 and 3, the result will be exaggerated valuations for the host country. As Ruitenbeek (1992) notes, the economics of invention reveals that income realised by inventors is considerably less than the ultimate value to society of the product, because the traits associated with the ultimate products have a very low degree of appropriability. This is true with respect to the countries providing niches to the diverse flora and fauna where the discoveries have to be made. This aberration in rent appropriation becomes even more blurred when the assumptions of ignorance, uncertainty, essentiality, and substitutability about medicinal plants enter the analysis. This implies that a factor representing the institutional framework should be applied to the ex-post discovery valuation. This factor will depend on the existence of the licensing structure in the host countries; whether research conducted in the host country causes other leakages in the economy; and whether the ability exists domestically to carry out the research. Thus this factor is expected to be low in tropical low income economies. In Ruitenbeek's terms:

$$CPV = a . EPV$$

where CPV is capturable production value and EPV is expected production value, ie the patent value of one discovery. The fact that *a* tends to be low explains why developing nations feel that the benefit of their efforts to conserve biodiversity is captured more by others. That is, *a*, can be thought of as a 'coefficient of rent capture'. One purpose of the 1992 Rio Biodiversity Convention is to raise the value of *a*.

The approach used here is fraught with difficulties given the considerable data deficiencies, but it is worth pursuing.

For any given area, say a hectare, there will be some probability, p, that the biodiversity 'supported' by that land will yield a successful drug D. Let the value of this drug be $V_i(D)$, where subscript i indicates one of two ways of estimating the value: the market price of the drug on the world market (i = 1), or the 'shadow' value of the drug which is determined by the number of lives that the drug saves and the value of a statistical life (i = 2). Since there are many other factors of production producing value in the drug, let r be the royalty that could be commanded if the host country could capture all the royalty value. Finally, let *a* be the coefficient of rent capture discussed previously. Then, the medicinal plant value of a hectare of 'biodiversity land' is:

$$V_{mp}(L) = p . r . a . V_i(D)$$

We will now consider each element of this equation in turn.

The probability of success: Principe (1989) estimates that the probability of any given plant species giving rise to a successful drug is between 1 in 10,000 and 1 in 1000. These estimates are based on discussions with drug company experts. Estimates of the number of plant species likely to be extinct in the next 50 years or so vary, but a figure of 60,000 is widely quoted. This suggests that somewhere between 6 and 60 of these species could have significant drug values. Put another way, if biodiversity use was favoured over alternative land uses, the realised benefit as far as medicinal drugs are concerned would be the economic value of these 6–60 species.

The royalty: based on the observation that existing royalty agreements involve royalties of 5–20%, but with a low figure for drug development some way into the future, we adopt a value of r = 0.05.

Rent capture: if host countries could capture rents perfectly then a = 1. Ruitenbeek (1992) suggests that rent capture is likely to be as low as 10% in low income countries. Hence a range for a is a = 0.1 to 1.0.

The value of drugs: Table 16 summarises some estimates of the value of successful drugs. The method of valuation is important because it affects the size of the estimate significantly. The valuation based on life-saving properties gives the highest values, using the value of a

Table 16 *The economic value of plant-based drugs*

	USA	OECD	World
		(billion $ 1990 prices)	
Market value of trade in medicinal plants	5.7 (1980)	17.2 (1981)	24.4? (1980)
Market or fixed value of plant-based drugs on prescription	11.7 (1985) 15.5 (1990)	35.1 (1985)	49.8? (1985)
Market value of prescription and over-the-counter plant-based drugs	19.8 (1985)	59.4 (1985)	84.3? (1985)
Value of plant-based drugs based on avoided deaths: anti-cancer only + non cancers	120.0 240.0 (1985)	360.0 720.0 (1985)	

Notes: Bracketed years are those for which values are estimated. Ratio of OECD to USA taken to be 3. 'Value of a statistical life' taken to be $4 million in 1990 prices. Lives saved taken to be 22,500–37,500 pa in USA. Average is taken here, ie 30,000. Multiply OECD by 1.4 to get to world estimates.

Source: adapted with modifications from Principe (1989)

'statistical life' of $4 million (Pearce, Bann and Georgiou, 1992). Market values of plant-based drugs give lower values, and the actual traded price of the plant material, the lowest value of all. The price of drugs reflects, of course, many more things than the cost of the plant source material. In that respect, the drug price grossly overstates the value of the plant. Equally, market prices understate true willingness to pay for drugs: there will be individuals who are willing to pay more than the market price for a given drug. Indeed, since the evidence suggests that such drugs tend to be price inelastic, this 'consumer surplus' element could be substantial. While there is no empirical basis for supposing that the consumer surplus element exactly offsets the overstatement in the price estimate, the two factors do work in opposite directions.

In the 1980s only about 40 plant species accounted for the plant-based prescribed drug sales in the USA. Thus, on the basis of prescription values only (Table 16), each species was responsible for $11.7 billion/40 = $290 million, on average. Since all life-saving drugs would be on prescription, use of the value of avoided deaths suggests a value per plant of $240 billion/40 = $6 billion per annum. Clearly, some species were far more valuable than others, but, taking the average it is possible to get some idea of the lost pharmaceutical value from disappearing species. If there are 60,000 species likely to be unavailable for medical research, and the probability that any given plant will produce a marketable prescription drug is 10^{-3} to 10^{-4}, then, taking a mean of 5×10^{-4} and applying it to the 60,000 estimated losses means that 30 plant-based drugs will be lost from species reduction. On market based figures, the *annual* loss to the USA alone would therefore be 30 × $292 million = $8.8 billion, and to OECD countries generally, perhaps $25 billion. In an update, Principe (1991) suggests that USA 1990 prescription plant-based medicines had a retail value of $15.5 billion, which would raise the value per plant to $390 million. As a benchmark, the GNP produced in the whole of Brazilian Amazonia is some $18 billion per annum. On the 'value of life approach' the *annual* losses would be 30 × $6 billion = $180 billion for the USA, and over $500 billion for the OECD countries generally. However, these figures assume that substitutes would not be forthcoming in the event that the plant species did become extinct.

Using the previous estimates it is possible to arrive at an estimate of the value of a 'representative' hectare of land. The model can now be written:

$$V_{mp}(L) = \{N_R \times p \times r \times a \times V_i/n\}/H \text{ per annum}$$

where the new notation is:

N_R = number of plant species at risk
n = number of drugs based on plant species
H = number of hectares of land likely to support medicinal plants
and
N_R = 60,000
p = 1/10,000 to 1/1000
r = 0.05
a = 0.1 to 1
V/n = 0.39 to 7.00 billion US$
H = 1 billion hectares, the approximate area of tropical forest left in the world.

The resulting range of values is from $0.01 to $21/ha. If a = 1 at all times, then the range is $0.1 to $21/ha. Clearly, the lower end of the range is negligible, but the upper end of the range would, for a discount rate of 5% and a long-time horizon amount to a present value of some $420/ha.

Ruitenbeek (1992) suggests an annual value of $85,000 (£50,000) for a = 1 for the Korup rainforest. The relevant area is either 126,000 ha (the central protected area) or 426,000 ha (the central area plus the surrounding management area), so that per hectare values would be $0.2 to $0.7 per hectare per annum, very much in keeping with the lower end of the range obtained from our own model.

In a study of medicinal plant harvesting in Belize, Balick and Mendelsohn (1992) estimate the *local* willingness to pay for land. Their annual net revenues are $19–61/ha. These values are not directly comparable to the estimates obtained above since they relate to local medicinal plant use rather than the 'global' commercial values to the OECD countries. It is significant, however, that they just overlap the upper range of the global values obtained above ($21 ha). Note also that such local values would be quickly depressed if very large tracts of land were devoted to medicinal plants, whereas the global values obtained here would be fairly invariant with supply since the existing supply already has many features of an open access resource.

Overall, then, despite the formidable data problems and the difficulties involved, the model used here does suggest values in a range from very low to around $20 per hectare.

The results are speculative and a great deal more research is needed. But the indication is clearly that the potential value of pharmaceuticals in the developing world could be very large. Nothing has been said about substitutes: if plant source material did not exist other substitutes would be available. If pharmaceutical companies thought plant source material was so important why have they not purchased large tracts of virgin forest? In terms of the concept of option value, however, the indications are that it might be substantial and in favour of conserving biological diversity on at least this ground.

Comparative economics of environmental conservation

Demonstrating the benefits of conservation is an essential part of the overall purpose of economic valuation. Conserving biological diversity is unlikely to succeed unless its economic value can be shown to be greater than the alternative land use. Some evidence is available to suggest that conservation in the sense of sustainable use of natural resources is, in many circumstances, to be preferred over conventional land uses (see box on page 90). But if this is so, why isn't the environment conserved automatically through market forces? The reasons why evidently superior market benefits for conservation uses are not realised in practice are complex. But a fundamental one is that market forces are very often not allowed to work in both developing *and* developed economies. Agriculture, for example, is subsidised world-wide, and especially in countries such as Japan, South Korea and the European Community. The result is that conservation has to compete not with the 'true' rate of return to the alternative land use but with a distorted rate of return, inflated by protectionist policies. This observation does much to explain why drawing of biodiversity 'conventions', while important, will achieve little. The basic require-ment has to be to correct and modify the economic policies that encourage people – farmers, industrialists, ordinary citizens – not to conserve. This issue is discussed at great length in Pearce and Warford (1992).

VALUATION AND GLOBAL ENVIRONMENTAL PROBLEMS

Valuing the damage from global warming clearly extends economic techniques into controversial and uncertain areas. In the first place, the sheer *scale* of global environmental issues is likely to make the

COMPARATIVE VALUES OF NATURAL HABITAT USE AND AGRICULTURAL PRODUCTION

Table 17 shows some estimates of the economic value of alternative land uses for developing countries. The evidence is limited but it contradicts the presumption that 'development' is always better than 'conservation'. If natural resources are managed wisely, and if people are allowed to exercise informed choices, conservation frequently pays in terms of conventional financial analysis.

Table 17 *Values of alternative land uses in developing countries*

Country	Use of habitat	Value (per ha)	Alternative use	Value
Kenya	Wildlife tourism	>>>	Cattle ranching	
Zimbabwe	Wildlife production	Z$4.2	Cattle ranching	Z$3.6
Malaysia	Forest production	$2455	Intensive agriculture	$217
Peru	Forest production	$6820	Clear-felling timber	$1000

Source: Swanson, T (1991) 'The Economics of Natural Habitat Utilisation: a Survey of the Literature and Issues' London Environmental Economics Centre (*mimeo*)

credibility of damage estimates suspect. Second, some global problems – such as global warming – may produce 'non-marginal' changes in well-being, whereas valuation techniques have been developed for comparatively small or 'marginal' effects. None the less there are several attempts to value global warming damage with the aim of throwing light on the setting of global warming 'targets', ie targets for the reduction in greenhouse gases. International agreements will aim to set some overall global target which will then be allocated between countries according to some 'burden sharing' formula.

Global warming damage is likely to show up in the form of forgone GNP and in 'non-GNP' costs. Existing studies are for the USA only: extension to the world requires some assumption about transferability

Table 18 *The economic damage from global warming*

	Present value (billion US$ 1990 pa) assuming a doubling of carbon dioxide equivalents	
	2050	2250
Agriculture	17.5	95.0
Forest loss	3.3	7.0
Sea level rise	7.0	35.0
Electricity requirements	11.7	67.0
Non-electric space heating	−1.3	−4.0
Human life	5.8	33.0
Hurricanes	0.8	6.4
Water supply	7.0	56.0
Urban infrastructure	0.1	0.6
Air pollution	3.5	19.8
Migration	0.5	2.8
Leisure activities	1.7	4.0
Species loss	4.0	16.0
Totals	61.6	338.6

Source: Cline, W (1991) *Estimating the Benefits of Greenhouse Warming Abatement* Paris, OECD

of US results to other economies. The results of one study are shown in Table 18. The estimated damage amounts to 1.1% of GNP. Expressed as a 'price' of a tonne of CO_2 the damage estimate is some $9 per tonne.

The estimates shown relate to damage done by doubling the concentration of CO_2 in the atmosphere $(2 \times CO_2)$, an outcome that, with 'trends continued', might occur around 2030–2050. The table also shows guesstimates for 2250 and these are substantially above those for 2050. The doubling level is merely a benchmark. If nothing is done by way of prevention, warming will continue. The 2250 estimates in fact correspond to a 10°C warming.

The estimates in Table 18 are part of ongoing work on the valuation of climate change effects. They are therefore provisional. But if damage done from the doubling of CO_2 concentrations amounts to around 1% of gross world product, then it is not as dramatic as some forecasters suggest and it is an appropriate area for the application of economic valuation techniques. Equally, the estimates make no allowance for dramatic change in the form of catastrophes etc. Finally, the estimates shown in Table 18 are *present values*: they have already been discounted, in this case using a discount rate of 1%. As noted previously, justifying such low discount rates on *conventional* efficiency grounds is probably not possible. Using 1% as a discount rate to reflect intergenerational equity is perhaps arbitrary but reflects the state of play. At rates of discount above 1% the 2250 damage estimate would be considerably reduced.

Chapter 5
Conclusions

Economic valuation is controversial largely because its purpose has not been clearly conveyed to non-economists. The purpose of valuation is to elicit measures of human preferences for or against environmental change. It is therefore immediately limited as a procedure by two issues. First, economic values are not the same as 'intrinsic' values, values 'in' things rather than values 'of' things. Economic valuation makes no claim to measure intrinsic values, although through the concept of 'existence' value, economic valuation may capture human perceptions of intrinsic value.

Second, measuring preferences focuses on the *efficiency* gains and losses from environmental change. It says little about the *distribution* of costs and benefits within a time period or between time periods. Within a time period the use of efficiency gains and losses as a guide to policy or project evaluation assumes that the prevailing distribution of income is socially acceptable, since it is that distribution which 'weights' the measures of willingness to pay. Between time periods, the use of a further efficiency concept – the discount rate – biases the outcomes of evaluation in favour of present and against future generations where costs and benefits in the future are both distant and significant. These are the broad 'limits' of valuation.

But economic valuation is useful in a number of contexts. Project and programme appraisal cannot be comprehensive or adequate without it. Setting national priorities for environmental policy is better informed if economic values are known with some degree of certainty. The entire objective of 'sustainable development' almost certainly cannot be interpreted without some idea of the value of environmental services and assets.

Empirical work on valuation remains limited, even in the developed world. It is fairly new in the developing world, although many project evaluations have used some form of indirect valuation. Its importance for the development process is that the revealed economic values for environmental conservation and environmentally improving projects and policies have frequently been found to be large. Valuation demonstrates that there is an economic case for protecting the environment, in addition to any ethical case. Valuation can assist the process of better decision-making. In so doing it offers the potential of more cost-efficient public choices, so that limited public income is spent to the best advantage.

Appendix I

Environmental policy as a constraint on economic growth

The focus of this book has been on the valuation of environmental impacts and one of the justifications for this focus is that environmental degradation frequently involves losses in GNP as conventionally measured. But policy-makers often have the opposite concern, namely that a stronger legislative stance will be at the expense of jobs, trade and inflation. Environmental policy is seen as a drag on economic growth. But these views rest on precious little empirical evidence, as this Appendix shows.

CURRENT SPENDING ON THE ENVIRONMENT

Figure 2 shows data on developed economy spending on environmental protection using data from the Organisation for Economic Cooperation and Development (OECD) in Paris. Despite the very imperfect database, it suggests that OECD nations spend around 1–1.5% of their GNP on environmental protection. Future costs are likely to be higher as the pressure to strengthen environmental policy grows and as international agreements expand (for example, on ozone layer protection, global warming, global biodiversity, tropical forest protection, toxic waste trade etc). To gain some idea of future costs, it is worth noting that the Netherlands *National Environmental Protection Plan*, one of the strictest in Europe, envisages spending of up to 3–4% of GNP.

The macroeconomic impact of environmental protection

A number of studies have been carried out on the costs of environmental protection in macroeconomic terms.

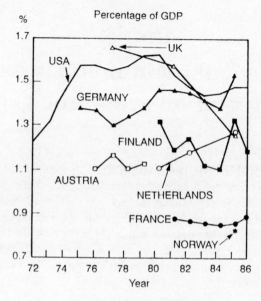

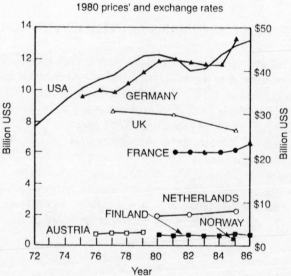

Figure 2 *Public and private expenditure on pollution control in OECD countries, 1972–86*
Notes: US figure refers to right-hand scale. Private household expenditure excluded.
1. Deflated with GDP price index
Source: OECD

United Kingdom

Barker and Lewney (1991) have simulated the macroeconomic impacts of three hypothetical environmental policies: a carbon tax designed to achieve the UK's conditional target of reducing CO_2 emissions back to their 1990 level by 2005; a fourfold rise in industrial pollution abatement expenditures by 2000; and an intensified water clean-up policy. The scenarios are run through the Cambridge Multisectoral Dynamic model. Table 19 shows the results of combining all three policies. As far as the carbon tax is concerned there are virtually no negative macroeconomic effects because of the use of VAT reductions to offset the carbon tax. This fiscal neutrality assumption is important. The pervasiveness of carbon fuels means that any tax has the potential to raise substantial government revenues. It may be therefore that any carbon tax regime would be fiscally neutral, with revenues being partly or wholly returned to the economy to offset deadweight losses from existing tax regimes, or as compensation for lower income groups who would be affected adversely by energy taxes. The overall result of this

Table 19 *Macroeconomic impacts of various environmental policies for the UK*

| | | Difference from base | | |
	1995	2000	2005	2010
GDP and Components of GDP				
(% difference from base)				
Consumer's expenditure	0.5	1.8	4.2	-1.7
Fixed investment	1.4	2.1	2.7	-1.3
Exports of goods and services	-0.1	-0.6	-1.2	-1.7
Imports of goods and services	0.4	0.5	1.1	-3.2
GDP at factor cost	0.4	0.9	2.2	-0.9
Inflation				
(pp difference from base)				
Consumer's prices	0.1	0.3	0.1	-0.2
Average earnings	0.3	0.6	0.7	-1.1
Employment				
(difference from base in '000s)				
Employment	191	427	682	0
Unemployment	-92	-207	-365	0

Source: Cambridge Econometrics

UK study is highly reassuring for the environmentalist. GDP is reduced from base levels by less than 1% in 2010, which translates to a reduction in growth rates of only 0.05% pa, and GDP actually increases before 2010. Unemployment falls by 2005 due to the rapid expansion of the pollution abatement industry, although this result is critically dependent on assumptions about full employment in the economy – a continuing debate among macroeconomists. In the Cambridge model, full employment is not achieved before 2005.

A separate simulation of a carbon tax using the Cambridge model has been run by Sondheimer (1991). This supposes a hypothetical tax of some £30 tonne carbon rising at the rate of inflation and offset by changes in direct and indirect taxes to secure approximate fiscal neutrality. Like the Barker–Lewney study, Sondheimer finds very little impact on GDP – a 0.5% reduction in baseline GDP – and a reduction in unemployment of some 70,000.

Ingham and Ulph (1990) have estimated the size of a carbon tax needed to secure 20% reductions on 1990 CO_2 emission levels by 2005 (stricter than the UK's stated target) and its macroeconomic effects. While the future tax is large (120–280% on coal in 2005, 60–130% on oil, and 16–71% on gas), they note that:

> the effects could be rather different from what is often supposed; in particular, any loss of competitiveness will be short-lived in terms of lost output, with a longer term boost to output due to enhanced productivity effects through scrapping of old equipment.

> (Ingham and Ulph, 1990)

As a result, manufacturing investment and employment actually *increase* rather dramatically. Assuming the economy grows at 2% pa, the carbon tax increases employment in 2005 by some 30% over the base case, and by 21% for a lower growth rate of 1% pa. Some runs of the model actually raise employment by over 100% compared to the base case. It needs to be noted that this result, while similar to the other studies, arises without the tax revenues being recycled back to the economy in the form of changes in other taxes.

While they vary in the degree of sophistication, the UK studies all suggest that environmental policy has a strong potential for *increasing* employment, or at least that it will not reduce it.

Norway

Norway has a strong tradition of using general equilibrium models to simulate policy measures. The Central Bureau of Statistics has regularly simulated the effects of environmental taxes since 1986. Glomsrod et al (1990) impose a hypothetical carbon tax designed to stabilise Norwegian CO_2 emissions at their 2000 level. The tax rises over time and in 2010 are approximately 100% higher than the price of fuel oil on a reference 'business as usual' scenario. The macroeconomic effects are that GDP growth is reduced from 2.7% pa to 2.3% pa; imports and exports show modest declines (down by 4–7% of what they otherwise would have been), while investment falls slightly (by around 1%).

The investment result is in total contrast to the Ingham–Ulph result, and arises from a change in the capital mix from shorter-life machinery to longer lived assets such as houses. Employment effects are not computed in aggregate, but work-hours in the pulp and paper sector and petroleum refining both fall significantly by 12–15%, but rise in housing, construction and textiles by similar amounts. Overall, the effects on employment appear negligible. This study is additionally notable for its attempt to estimate the *benefits* of such a policy. It suggests that the cost to Norway of some 27 billion krone (1986 prices) is considerably recouped by some 19.1 billion krone of health benefits and reduced congestion, noise, accidents and road damage.

Netherlands

The Netherlands has produced one of the most detailed environmental policy statements of any country – the *National Environmental Policy Plan* (1989). The policy involves a doubling of environmental protection expenditures as a proportion of GDP, substantial increases in energy conservation, investment in public transport and constraints on the use of private vehicles, waste recycling and reduced fertiliser use. Table 20 shows the results of the NEPP in terms of its macroeconomic impacts. GNP rises by 95% compared to 98% by 2010 compared to 1985, a slowdown of under 0.1% pa, but may actually increase if other countries pursue similar policies. Employment is seen to be unaffected, and could even rise if other countries respond with similar policies.

Table 20 *Macroeconomic impacts of a strong environmental policy: the Netherlands*

| | Results in 2010 (compared to 1985) | Sustainable growth | |
	Unchanged policy	without[1]	with[2]
Volume GNP (%)	+98	+95	+100
Real wages (%)	+61	+59	+61
Consumption (%)	+119	+118	+121
Budget deficit (% point of NI)	+26	+26	+28
Interest point (% point)	-2.4	+1.0	-3.4
CO_2 emissions (%)	-1.1	+0.2	-0.7
CFCs emissions (%)	+35	-20 to	-30
SO_2 emissions (%)	-100	-100	
NO_x emissions (%)	-50	-80 to	-90
Hydrocarbons (%)	-10	-70 to	-80
Discharges into Rhine and North Sea (%)	-20	-70 to	-80
	-50	-75	
Waste dumping (%)	0	-70 to	-80
Environmental expenditure (% NI)	2	4	
Total investment 1985–2010	100	350	

Notes:
1 Without equivalent policy in foreign countries
2 With equivalent policy in foreign countries

Source: NEPP, 1989

The European Community

The OECD's INTERLINK country forecasting model has been used to simulate the effects of the European Community's Large Combustion Plants Directive which requires significant reductions in emission of sulphur and nitrogen oxides from power stations and large industrial boilers (Klaassen et al, 1987). The investments in pollution control equipment and plant modification necessary to achieve the targets have the effect of *increasing* GDP and employment in the immediate five years after the assumed implementation of the Directive. Longer-term adjustment involves some slight reduction in GDP and employment. The results are shown in Table 21. The overwhelming impression is once again that restrictions on air pollutants have very little impact on

Table 21 *Income and employment impacts of acid rain pollution control in the European Community*

| | Annual % deviation from baseline levels | | | |
| | Control of SO_2 | | Control of NO_x | |
	1988–93	1994–7	1988–93	1994–7
France				
GDP	0.04	0.03	na	na
Employment	0.02	0.02	na	na
Germany				
GDP	0.13	–0.06	0.06	0.00
Employment	0.13	–0.11	0.05	–0.03
Italy				
GDP	0.08	0.03	0.03	0.02
Employment	0.02	0.01	0.01	0.01
UK				
GDP	0.06	–0.05	0.01	–0.01
Employment	0.03	–0.05	0.01	–0.01

Source: Klaassen et al, 1987

income and employment. The investment in pollution abatement equipment tends to expand the economy. As higher pollution control costs work their way through the economy, so prices do rise to some extent and deflate the economy slightly, an effect reinforced by the cessation of the extra investment once abatement measures are complete.

The USA

US studies of the effects of environmental regulation are more plentiful. Hahn and Hird (1991) assemble estimates of the costs of regulation generally, both economic regulation (eg of trade) and social regulation (eg of environmental damage). Economic regulations tend to have very limited economic benefits. Hahn and Hird estimate that such measures cost the US economy some $46 billion each year. Social regulation costs between $78 billion and $107 billion, but yields benefits of some $42–181 billion. Environmental regulation dominates social regulation, accounting for some 70% of the cost and some 40–75% of benefits. Hahn and Hird suggest that environmental control costs are probably slightly above the benefits to the US economy.

Reference to the benefits of environmental policy serves as a caution to 'straight' macroeconomic impact studies. For example, environmental policy benefits health and hence probably contributes to productivity. These effects need to be seen as offsets to the direct 'GDP costs' of environmental regulation. Probably the most detailed study of environmental regulation costs in the USA is that by Jorgensen and Wilcoxen (1990), but this study does not make any allowance for the feedback effect from health benefits. The study simulates the past effects of US environmental policy on economic growth between 1973 and 1985 through a long-term growth model. The annual GDP growth rate for the period is found to have *fallen* by 0.19 percentage points because of the 'drag' effects of environmental regulation. This amounts to something like twice the magnitude being suggested for non-USA studies. The difference could reflect either the nature of US environmental regulation, or the difference in the modelling procedure. Converted to a long-run projection, the Jorgensen–Wilcoxen model suggests that GDP might be some 2.6% lower as a result of regulation. The model results do not indicate the effects on employment, but clearly they would tend to be negative.

Nordhaus (1991b) has looked at the broad impacts of all 'resource scarcity' on world economic growth. He estimates that rising energy prices probably constitute a 'drag' of about 0.15% pa and that greenhouse warming will add a further 0.03% to this. Allowing for other environmental and mineral scarcity costs, the total drag is tentatively put at 0.31% pa, ie a hypothetical GDP growth of 3% pa would become 2.7% pa. But the costs of environmental policy are not a major part of this cost on Nordhaus's estimates. If the Jorgensen–Wilcoxen estimate is applied to the world (a clear exaggeration given the relative strictness of US environmental policy) the 0.31% estimate might rise to 0.45%, which begins to look significant.

OECD

The OECD has published the results of a six-country survey of environmental policy costs (OECD, 1985). Covering the USA, Norway, the Netherlands, France, Finland and Austria, the study concluded that the effects of policy on GDP were indeterminate, with long-run rises of 1% over baseline in some cases and falls of 1% in others; that inflation might generally be worsened by as much as 0.3–0.5% pa; that employment is *stimulated* by the growth of the pollution abatement sector and a slight depressing effect on productivity; and that the beneficial effects of increased regulatory expenditures occur in the short-term, with the negative effects occurring in the longer-run. The OECD concludes that:

> While these various results are of interest in their own right, the main conclusion which emerges from them is that the macroeconomic effect of environmental policies is relatively small. Most of the figures reported – with the exception of some of the results for consumer price inflation – are in the range of a few tenths of a percentage point per year. Furthermore, it is important to recall that these small effects were registered during a period (the 1970s) of peak pollution control activity, when efforts were directed not only at limiting on-going pollution, but also at cleaning-up the backlog caused by neglect of the environment during the 1950s and 1960s.
>
> (OECD, 1985)

CONCLUSIONS

The available economic studies do not bear out the worst fears about the employment, price and income effects of environmental policy. They tend to suggest that environmental policy can actually *increase* employment and income, or at least make them no worse with regulation compared to the situation without it. But there are several caveats. First, the detailed study by Jorgensen and Wilcoxen for the USA suggests annual GDP 'sacrifices' that politicians would probably regard as being significant. How far this result reflects specific US regulatory measures and how far it reflects the sophistication of the macroeconomic model is impossible to say. Second, these sacrifices have to be compared to the benefits of environmental policy, on which there is even less empirical evidence. Third, the relevant studies are still limited in number. The fact that regulatory impacts take some time to work through the economy also means that the methodologies involved require longer-run economic growth models than those typically used for short-term forecasting. But we can be sure that the evidence available does *not* support the political received wisdom that more environmental regulation will be harmful to economic growth, at least in Europe. Finally, whatever the cost of environmental policy, there ought to be more emphasis on *efficiency* in policy, and that tends to point towards a bolder policy of embracing green taxes and tradeable permit systems to supplement traditional regulatory policies.

Appendix II
Monetary valuation techniques

There are four broad categories of valuation technique that have been developed to a sophisticated level.

CONVENTIONAL MARKET APPROACHES

These approaches use market prices for the environmental service that is affected, or, if market prices are not an accurate guide to scarcity, then they may be adjusted by *shadow pricing*. Where environmental damage or improvement shows up in changes in the quantity or price of *marketed* inputs or outputs, the value of the change can be measured by changes in the total 'consumers plus producers surplus'. If the changes are small the monetary measure can be approximated by *market* values. The following two approaches may be distinguished.

1   The *dose-response* approach. Under this approach a given level of pollution, say, is associated with a change in output and that output is valued at market or shadow prices.
2   The *replacement cost* technique. This technique looks at the cost of replacing or restoring a damaged asset and uses this cost as a measure of the benefit of restoration. It needs to be used with some care (see below).

Examples of market pricing approaches include the costs of cleaning buildings made dirty by air pollution; the loss of crop output from air pollution; and clean-up costs downstream from water pollution upstream. Other valuation approaches use market values but they are classified separately here (eg the avertive behaviour approach).

HOUSEHOLD PRODUCTION FUNCTIONS (HPFs)

In the HPF approach expenditures on commodities that are *substitutes* or *complements* for the environmental characteristic are used to value changes in that environmental characteristic. Thus, noise insulation is a substitute for a reduction in noise at source; travel is a complement to the recreational experience at the recreation site (it is necessary to travel to experience the recreational benefit). There are two types of HPF approach, as follows.

1 *Avertive expenditures*, by which expenditures on the various substitutes for the environmental change are added together.
2 *The travel cost method*, by which expenditures on the travel needed to reach the recreational site can be interpreted to give an estimate of the benefit arising from the recreational experience.

HEDONIC PRICE METHODS (HPM)

With HPM an attempt is made to estimate an *implicit price* for environmental attributes by looking at real markets in which those characteristics are effectively traded. Thus, 'clean air' and 'peace and quiet' are effectively traded in the property market since purchasers of houses and land do consider these environmental dimensions as characteristics of property. The attribute 'risk' is traded in the labour market. High risk jobs may well have 'risk premia' in the wages to compensate for the risk. The two HPM markets of most interest, therefore, are:

1 *hedonic house (land) prices*, for valuing air quality, noise, neighbourhood features (parks etc); and
2 *wage risk premia*, for valuing changes in morbidity and mortality arising from environmental (and safety) hazards.

EXPERIMENTAL METHODS

With experimental approaches a direct attempt is made to elicit preferences by questionnaire ('structured conversations'). Two kinds of questioning may take place, as follows.

1 Eliciting *values*. Here a direct attempt is made to ask 'what are you willing to pay for X or to prevent Y' and/or 'what are you willing to accept to forgo Z or tolerate A'. This is the *contingent valuation method* (CVM).
2 Eliciting *rankings*. Here the questioner is content to obtain a ranking of preferences which can later be 'anchored' by the analyst in a real

price of something observed in the market. This is the *contingent ranking* (CRM) or *stated preference* (SP) method.

Some valuation procedures are widely used but their interpretation as changes in consumers/producers surplus is not straightforward.

Replacement cost

The replacement cost approach is straightforward. If environmental damage is done, it is often possible to find out quite easily the cost of restoring the damaged environment. The replacement cost is often widely used to measure the damage. The approach is correct where it is possible to argue that the remedial work *must* take place because of some other constraint. Such situations will be quite widespread. For example, where there is a water quality standard that is mandatory, then the costs of achieving that standard are a proxy for the benefits of reaching the standard. This is because society can be construed as having sanctioned the cost by setting the standard.

There are risks in this procedure. If the remedial cost is a measure of damage then the cost-benefit ratio of undertaking the remedial work will always be unity: remedial costs are being used to measure remedial benefits. To say that the remedial work must be done implies that benefits exceed costs, whatever the latter are. Costs are then a *minimum* measure of benefits. If, to pursue the water quality example, the standard has clearly been set without thought for costs, then using replacement costs as a measure of minimum benefits could be misleading. A standard based on 'BATNEEC' tends to fit the replacement cost approach, but others may not. Judgement is required, as with many valuation problems.

Another situation where the replacement cost approach is valid would be where there is an overall constraint not to let environmental quality decline (sometimes called a 'sustainability constraint'). In these circumstances replacement costs might be allowable as a first approximation of benefits or damage. The so-called *shadow project* approach relies on such constraints. It argues that the cost of any project designed to restore an environment because of a sustainability constraint is then a minimum valuation of the damage done.

Opportunity cost technique

On the opportunity cost approach no direct attempt is made to value benefits. Instead, the benefits of the activity causing environmental deterioration – say, a housing development – are estimated in order to set a benchmark for what the environmental benefits *would have to be* for the development *not* to be worthwhile. Clearly, this is not a valuation technique but, properly handled, it can be a powerful approach to a form of judgemental valuation. It has been particularly useful in evaluations of energy and mining developments.

Any environmental asset is capable of being characterised by several types of economic value. To ensure that the valuation exercise is carried out properly it is necessary to check that all components have been assessed. The components are discussed in the main text and are:

User values + Non-user values = Total economic value

User values, as the name implies, relate to the preferences that people have for using the environmental asset in question, eg value of fishing in a river, value of recreation at a beach site, value of breathing clean air, etc. *Non-user* values arise when the asset is valued by people who make no direct use of the asset. Many people care about the African elephant or an ecologically precious wetland without having seen either. If they value the asset because they think they would probably like to see it one day, then this is an *option value* – a kind of insurance payment to make sure the asset still exists at the time the individual decides he or she will exercise the choice of using it. Many people value things like elephants and wetlands even though they have not seen them in their 'natural' state, nor do they plan to see them. Such people are expressing *existence value*.

Whether option value is regarded as a use or non-use value or not, matters little. The *total economic value* will therefore comprise:

TEV = User values + Option values + Existence values

When are option and existence values likely to be important? The evidence suggests that they are potentially very important when the damage done or threat is to a *unique* or very *well known* environmental asset (the Grand Canyon, Broads area, Flow country, endangered species etc). In such circumstances it is very important that non-use values be investigated. From the brief outline of techniques above, it will be evident that *only the experimental market approach can capture non-use values*. This is why so much recent valuation work has used CVM (and to a lesser extent CRM/SP).

VALUATION TECHNIQUES IN OUTLINE

The following brief sections describe each technique and its pros and cons.

'Validity' might be assessed in the following terms.

Theoretical validity – is the technique consistent with the underlying theory of surplus measurement?

Convergent validity – do the results of studies using each technique have the expected relationship with the results of using other studies? For example, different theoretically valid techniques should give similar estimates of willingness to pay (WTP) or willingness to accept (WTA), but we have no particular reason to say any one technique is 'correct'. In the convergent validity test, then, we check to see if, say, HPM and CVM give similar results. If they do, that should contribute to the credibility of the results.

Repetitive validity – does the same technique applied to *similar* contexts yield broadly similar values? This test is weak in that there is no *a priori* reason why the value of, say, a wetland in the UK should be the same as one in Spain, even after correcting for income differences. Tastes may simply vary. Nonetheless, it offers a little more information. The extent to which values in one place can be *transferred* to another place is, as yet, under-researched.

Criterion validity – does the technique yield results that bear a consistent relationship with real market behaviour?

MARKET VALUE APPROACHES

Range of applicability

Extensively used where 'dose-response' relationships between pollution and output or impact are known. Examples include crop and forest damage from air pollution, materials damage, health impacts of pollution. Limited to cases where there are markets, ie cannot estimate non-use values. Replacement cost approaches also widely used because it is often relatively easy to find estimates of such costs. Replacement cost approaches should be confined to situations where the cost relates to achieving some agreed environmental standard, or where there is an overall constraint requiring that a certain level of environmental quality is achieved.

Procedure

Dose-response: take physical and ecological links between pollution ('dose') and impact ('response') and value the final impact at a market or shadow price. Most of the effort usually resides in the non-economic exercise of establishing the dose-response links. Multiple regression techniques often used for this.

Replacement cost: ascertain environmental damage and then estimate cost of restoring environment to its original state.

Validity

Dose-response: theoretically a sound approach. Uncertainty resides mainly in the errors in the dose-response relationship: eg where, if at all, are threshold levels before damage occurs; are there 'jumps' (discontinuities) in the dose-damage relationship? An adequate 'pool' of studies may not be available for cross-reference.
Criterion validity is not relevant since presence of 'real' markets tends to be a test in itself, ie revealed preferences in the market place are being used as the appropriate measure of value.

Replacement cost: validity limited to contexts where agreed standards must be met.

Expense

Dose-response can be costly if large databases need to be manipulated in order to establish dose-response relationships. If dose–response functions already exist, this method can be very inexpensive and with low time demands.

Replacement cost is usually very inexpensive as standard engineering data often exist.

Case study US Environmental Protection Agency (1985) *Costs and Benefits of Reducing Lead in Gasoline: Final Regulatory Impact Analysis* EPA-230-05-85-006, Washington DC, February.

HOUSEHOLD PRODUCTION FUNCTIONS I:
AVERTIVE EXPENDITURES

Range of
applicability
Limited to cases where households spend money to offset environmental hazards, but these can be important, eg noise insulation expenditures; risk-reducing expenditures such as smoke-detectors, safety belts, water filters etc.

Has not been used to estimate non-use values though arguable that payments to some wildlife societies can be interpreted as insurance payments for conservation.

Procedure
Whilst used comparatively rarely, the approach is potentially important. Expenditures undertaken by households and designed to offset some environmental risk need to be identified. Examples include noise abatement, reactions to radon gas exposure, eg purchase of monitoring equipment, visits to medics etc. Technique needs to be managed by experts as significant econometric modelling is usually required.

Validity
Theoretically correct. Insufficient studies to comment on convergent validity. Uses actual expenditures so criterion validity is generally met.

Expense
Econometric analysis on panel and survey data usually needed. Fairly expensive.

Case study
Dickie, M, Gerking, S and Agee, M (1991) 'Health Benefits of Persistent Micropollutant Control: the Case of Stratospheric Ozone Depletion and Skin Damage Risks' in J B Opschoor and D W Pearce (eds) *Persistent Pollutants: Economics and Policy* Kluwer, Dordrecht.

HOUSEHOLD PRODUCTION FUNCTIONS II: TRAVEL COST METHOD

Range of applicability Generally limited to *site* characteristics and to valuation of time. Former tends to be recreational sites. Latter often known as *discrete choice*, eg implicit value of time can be estimated by observing how choice between travel modes is made or how choice of good relates to travel time avoided (last case has been used to value women's water collection time in developing countries).

Cannot be used to estimate non-use values.

Procedure Detailed sample survey needed of travellers, together with their costs of travel to the site. Complications include possible benefits of the travelling, and presence of competing sites.

Validity Theoretically correct, but complicated where there are competing sites and multi-purpose trips. Some doubts about 'construct validity' in that number of trips should be inversely correlated with 'price' of trips, ie distance travelled. Some UK studies do not show this relationship. Convergent validity generally good in US studies. Generally very acceptable to official agencies and conservation groups.

Case study Willis, K and Benson, J (1988) 'Valuation of Wildlife: A Case Study on the Upper Teesdale Site of Special Scientific Interest and Comparison of Methods in Environmental Economics' in R K Turner (ed) *Sustainable Environmental Management: Principles and Practice* Belhaven Press, London.

HEDONIC PRICING I: HOUSE PRICE METHOD

Range of applicability   Applicable only to environmental attributes likely to be capitalised into the price of housing and/or land. Most relevant to noise and air pollution and neighbourhood amenity.

Does not measure non-use value and is confined to cases where property owners are aware of environmental variables and act because of them (as with avertive behaviour).

Procedure   Approach generally involves assembly of cross sectional data on house sales or house price estimates by estate agents, together with data on factors likely to influence these prices. Multiple regression techniques are then needed to obtain the first estimate of an 'implicit price'. Technically, a further stage of analysis is required since the multiple regression approach does not identify the demand curve directly. Often this stage of the analysis is omitted because of complexity.

Validity   Theoretically sound, although final estimate is not of a demand curve as such (see above). Markets often may not behave as required by the approach. Data on prices and factors determining prices often difficult to come by. Limited tests of convergent validity but reveals encouraging results.

Case study   Brookshire, D et al (1982) 'Valuing Public Goods: A Comparison of Survey and Hedonic Approaches' *American Economic Review*, vol 72, no 1.

HEDONIC PRICING II: WAGE RISK METHODS

Range of applicability Limited to valuation of morbidity and mortality risks in occupations. Resulting 'values of life' have been widely used and applied elsewhere, eg in the dose-response approach.

Procedure As with HPM, the approach uses multiple regression to relate wages/salaries to factors influencing them. Included in the determining factors is a measure of risk of accident. The resulting 'wage premium' can then be related to risk factors to derive a so-called value of a statistical life.

Validity Theoretically sound. Convergent validity may be tested against CVM of risk reduction, but wage-risk approach measures WTA not WTP.

Case study Marin, A and Psacharopoulos, G (1982) 'The Reward for Risk in the Labour Market: Evidence from the United Kingdom and a Reconciliation with Other Studies' *Journal of Political Economy*, vol 90.

EXPERIMENTAL MARKETS I: CONTINGENT VALUATION

Range of applicability

Extensive since it can be used to derive values for almost any environmental change. This explains its attractiveness to 'valuers'. Only method for eliciting non-use values.

Procedure

The method involves setting up a carefully worded questionnaire which asks people their WTP and/or WTA through structured questions. Various forms of 'bidding game' can be devised involving 'yes/no' answers to questions and statements about maximum WTP. Resulting survey results need econometric analysis to derive mean values of WTP bids. Literature tends to suggest that most sensible results come from cases where respondents are familiar with the asset being 'valued'.

Validity

The literature has identified various forms of potential bias. 'Strategic bias' arises if respondents make bids that do not reflect their 'true' values. They may do this if they think there is a 'free rider' situation. But there is limited evidence of strategic bias. Hypothetical bias arises because respondents are not making 'real' transactions. Expense usually limits the number of experiments involving real money (criterion validity), but some studies exist. Convergent validity is good. Construct validity – relating values to expectations about values of other measures – is debated, especially the marked divergence in many studies between WTP and WTA.

Case study

Case material is extensively reviewed in Mitchell, R and Carson, R (1989) *Using Surveys to Value Public Goods: the Contingent Valuation Method* Resources for the Future, Washington DC.

EXPERIMENTAL MARKETS II:
CONTINGENT RANKING

Range of applicability   Unknown but could be extensive. Limited number of studies exist for environmental context and are confined to 'private goods', ie goods purchased in the market place. It is unclear how extensive the application could be for environmental goods but this is under investigation in the context of house location decisions.

Procedure   Individuals are asked to rank several alternatives rather than express a WTP. Alternatives tend to differ according to some risk characteristic and price. Idea could be extended to a ranking of house characteristics with some 'anchor' such as the house price being used to convert rankings into WTP.

Validity   Not widely discussed in the literature but appears theoretically valid. Too few studies to test other validity measures but initial results suggest CRM WTP exceeds CVM WTP.

Case study   Margat, W, Viscusi, W and Huber, J (1987) 'Paired Comparisons and Contingent Valuation Approaches to Morbidity Risk Valuation' *Journal of Environmental Economics and Management*, vol 15.

Bibliography

Adger, N and Whitby, M (1991) 'National Accounting for the Externalities of Agriculture and Forestry' Countryside Change Unit, University of Newcastle-upon-Tyne, Working Paper 16, April

Anderson, D (1987) *The Economics of Afforestation: a Case Study in Africa* Johns Hopkins University Press, Baltimore

Anderson, D (1989) 'Economic Aspects of Afforestation and Soil Conservation Projects', in G Schramm and J Warford *Environmental Management and Economic Development* Johns Hopkins University Press, Baltimore

Balick, M and Mendelsohn, R (1992) 'Assessing the Economic Value of Traditional Medicines from Tropical Rain Forests' Conservation Biology, vol 6, no 1, March

Barbier, E, Burgess, J, Swanson, T and Pearce, D W (1990) *Elephants, Economics and Ivory* Earthscan, London

Barbier, E et al (1991) *Economic Valuation of Wetland Benefits: the Hadeja-Jama'are Floodplain, Nigeria* London Environmental Economics Centre, Paper 91–02, London

Barde, J-Ph and Pearce, D W (eds) (1991) *Valuing the Environment* Earthscan, London

Barker, T and Lewney, R (1991) 'A Green Scenario for the UK Economy', in T Barker (ed) *Green Futures for Economic Growth: Britain in 2010* Cambridge Econometrics, Cambridge

Bennett, J (1982) 'Using Direct Questioning to Value Existence Benefits of Preserved Natural Areas' School of Business Studies, Darling Downs Institute of Education, Toowoomba

Bergstrom, J et al (1990) 'Economic Value of Wetlands-Based Recreation' *Ecological Economics*, vol 2, no 2, June

Bishop, J (1990) *The Cost of Soil Erosion in Malawi* Report to Malawi Country Operations Department, World Bank, November

Bishop, J and Allen, J (1989) *The On-Site Costs of Soil Erosion in Mali* Environment Department Working Paper No 21, November, World Bank, Washington DC

Boulding, K (1966) 'The Economics of the Coming Spaceship Earth', in H Jarrett (ed) *Environmental Quality in a Growing Economy* Johns Hopkins University Press, Baltimore

Boyle, K and Bishop, R (1985) 'The Total Value of Wildlife Resources: Conceptual and Empirical Issues' Paper presented to Association of Environmental and Resource Economists, Boulder, May

Braden, J and Kolstad, C (eds) (1991) *Measuring the Demand for Environmental Quality* North Holland, Amsterdam (This is a technically difficult volume for the professionals only, but is by far the best exposition of the analytical foundations and results of monetary valuation.)

Briscoe, J, de Castro, P, Griffin, C, North, J and Olsen, O (1990) 'Toward Equitable and Sustainable Rural Water Supplies: a Contingent Valuation Study in Brazil' *The World Bank Economic Review*, vol 4, no 2

Brookshire, D et al (1983) 'Estimating Option Prices and Existence Values for Wildlife Resources' *Land Economics*, 59

Brookshire, D, Schulze, W and Thayer, M (1985) 'Some Unusual Aspects of Valuing a Unique Natural Resource' Department of Economics, University of Wyoming, February (*mimeo*)

Broome, J (1991) *The Intergenerational Aspects of Climate Change* Report to the UK Economic and Social Research Council, Swindon

Brown, G and Hall, W (1989) *The Viewing Value of Elephants* London Environmental Economics Centre, London

Clark, W 'Economics and Marketing of Canada's Capistrano' in A Diamond and F Filion (eds) (1987) *The Value of Birds* International Council for Bird Preservation, Cambridge

Cline, W (1991) *Estimating the Benefits of Greenhouse Warming Abatement* OECD, Paris

Costanza, R, Farber, S and Maxwell, J (1989) 'Valuation and Management of Wetland Ecosystems' *Ecological Economics* vol 1, no 4, December

Dahle, L et al (1987) 'Attitudes Towards and Willingness to Pay for Brown Bear, Wolverine and Wolf in Norway' Department of Forest Economics, Agricultural University of Norway, Report 5/1987 (in Norwegian)

Dasgupta, P Sen, A and Marglin, S (1972) *Guidelines for Project Evaluation* UNIDO, Vienna

Gittinger, H (1982) *Economic Analysis of Agricultural Projects* Johns Hopkins University Press, Baltimore

Glomsrod, S, Vennemo, H and Johnson, T (1990) 'Stabilisation of Emissions of CO_2: a Computable General Equilibrium Assessment' Central Bureau of Statistics, Oslo, Discussion Paper no 48, April

Hageman, R (1985) 'Valuing Marine Mammal Populations: Benefit Valuations in a Multi-Species Ecosystem' National Marine Fisheries Service, Southwest Fisheries Center, Report LJ-85-22, La Jolla, California

Hahn, R and Hird, J (1991) 'The Costs and Benefits of Regulation: Review and Synthesis' *Yale Journal of Regulation*, vol 8, no 1, winter

Hervik, A et al (1986) 'Implicit Costs and Willingness to Pay for Development of Water Resources' in Carlsen, A (ed) *Proceedings of UNESCO Symposium on Decision Making in Water Resources Planning*, May, Oslo

Imber, D et al (1991) *A Contingent Valuation Survey of the Kakadu Conservation Zone* Resource Assessment Commission, Research Paper no 3, Canberra, February

Ingham, A and Ulph, A (1990) 'Carbon Taxes and the UK Manufacturing Sector' Department of Economics, University of Southampton (*mimeo*)

Jacquemot, A and Filion, F (1987) 'The Economic Significance of Birds in Canada' in A Diamond and F Filion (eds) *The Value of Birds* International Council for Bird Preservation, Cambridge

Johansson, P-O (1987) *The Economic Theory and Measurement of Environmental Benefits* Cambridge University Press, Cambridge (A technical volume but a bit easier going than Braden and Kolstad)

Jorgensen, D and Wilcoxen, P (1990) 'Environmental Regulation and US Economic Growth', *RAND Journal of Economics* vol 21, no 2 summer

Klaassen, G, Kee, P, Nentjes, A, Hafkamp, W and Olsthoorn, A (1987) *The Macroeconomic Effects of the Large Combustion Plants Directive Proposal: Economic Aspects of Controlling Acid Rain in Europe* Institute for Environmental Studies, Free University of Amsterdam, Amsterdam

Little, I M D and Mirrlees, J (1974) *Project Appraisal and Planning for Developing Countries* Heinemann, London

McGrath, W and Arens, P (1989) *The Costs of Soil Erosion on Java: a Natural Resource Accounting Approach* World Bank, Environment Department Working Paper 15, Washington, August

Mu, X, Whittington, D, Briscoe, J (1989) 'Modeling Village Water Demand Behavior: a Discrete Choice Approach' *Water Resources Research* vol 26, no 4

Navrud, S (1991) 'Norway', in J-Ph Barde and Pearce, D W *Valuing the Environment* Earthscan, London

Nelson, J (1980) 'Airports and Property Values: a Survey of Recent Evidence' *Journal of Transport Economics and Policy*, XIV

Nelson, J (1982) 'Highway Noise and Property Values: a Survey of Recent Evidence' *Journal of Transport Economics and Policy*, XVI

Netherlands Ministry of Housing, Physical Planning and the Environment (1989) *National Environmental Policy Plan of the Netherlands*, Amsterdam (This policy was updated by 'NEPP+' in 1990 which committed further funding for energy conservation and some other measures)

Newcombe, K (1989) 'An Economic Justification for Rural Afforestation: the Case of Ethiopia' in G Schramm and J Warford (eds) *Environmental Management and Economic Development* Johns Hopkins University Press, Baltimore

Nordhaus, W (1991) 'Economic Growth: Limits and Perils' Paper presented to the International Congress on Environment, Ethics, Economics and Institutions Milan, March

Nordhaus, W (1991) 'A Sketch of the Economics of the Greenhouse Effect' *American Economic Review*, vol 81, no 2

OECD (1985) *The Macroeconomic Impact of Environmental Expenditure* OECD, Paris

OECD (1989) *Environmental Policy Benefits: Monetary Valuation* OECD, Paris

Opschoor, J (1986) 'A Review of Monetary Estimates of Benefits of Environmental Improvement in the Netherlands' OECD, Paris, October

Ottinger, R et al (1990) *Environmental Costs of Electricity* PACE University Center for Environmental Legal Studies, White Plains, New York, September

Pearce, D W (ed) (1991) *Blueprint 2* Earthscan, London

Pearce, D W (ed) (forthcoming) *Blueprint 3*, Earthscan, London

Pearce, D W and Atkinson, G (1992a) *Are National Economics Sustainable? Measuring Sustainable Development* CSERGE, University College London

Pearce, D, Bann, C and Georgiou, S (1992b) *The Social Cost of Fuel Cycles* HMSO, London

Pearce, D W and Markandya, A (1987) *Environmental Policy Benefits: Monetary Valuation* OECD, Paris (A general overview with empirical results. Difficult material is relegated to annexes.)

Pearce, D W, Markandya, A and Barbier, E (1989) *Blueprint for a Green Economy* Earthscan, London

Pearce, D W, Moran, D and Fripp, E (1992c) 'The Economic Value of Biological and Cultural Diversity' Report to the World Conservation Union, CSERGE, University College, London

Pearce, D W and Warford, J (1993) *World Without End: Economic Environment and Sustainable Development* Oxford University Press, New York and Oxford

Portney, P (ed) (1990) *Public Policies for Environmental Protection* Resources for the Future, Washington DC

Principe, P (1989) 'The Economic Significance of Plants and their Constituents as Drugs' in H Wagner, H Hikino and N Farnsworth *Economic and Medicinal Plant Research*, vol 3, London, Academic Press, pp 1–17

Repetto, R (1989) *Wasting Assets – Natural Resources in the National Income Accounts* World Resources Institute, Washington

Ruitenbeek, J (1990a) 'The Rainforest Supply Price: a Step Towards Estimating a Cost Curve for Rainforest Conservation' Suntory-Toyota International Centre for Economics and Related Disciplines, Paper 29, London School of Economics, September

Ruitenbeek, J (1990b) *Evaluating Economic Policies for Promoting Rainforest Conservation in Developing Countries*, PhD thesis, London School of Economics

Ruitenbeek, J (1990c) *Economic Analysis of Tropical Forest Conservation Initiatives: Examples from West Africa* World Wide Fund for Nature, Godalming

Ruitenbeek, J (1992) 'The Rainforest Supply Price: a Tool for Evaluating Rainforest Conservation Expenditures' *Ecological Economics* vol 6, no 1, July, pp 57–78

Samples, K et al (1986) 'Information Disclosure and Endangered Species Valuation' *Land Economics*, vol 62, no 3

Schulz, W (1986) 'A Survey of the Status of Research Concerning the Benefits of Environmental Policy in the Federal Republic of Germany' OECD, Paris

Schulze, W et al (1983) 'The Economic Benefits of Preserving Visibility in the National Parklands of the Southwest' *Natural Resources Journal*, vol 23, January

Sondheimer, J (1991) 'Macroeconomic Effects of a Carbon Tax', in Barker and Lewney

Squire, L and van der Tak, H (1975) *Economic Analysis of Projects* Johns Hopkins University Press, Baltimore

Stoll, R and Johnson, L (1984) 'Concepts of Value, Non-market Valuation, and the Case of the Whooping Crane' Department of Agricultural Economics, Texas A&M University

Thibodeau, F and Ostro, B (1981) 'An Economic Analysis of Wetland Protection' *Journal of Environmental Management*, 12 (1), January

Thomas, D et al (1990) 'Use Values and Non-Use Values in the Conservation of Ichkeul National Parl, Tunisia' Department of Geography, University College London, London (*mimeo*)

Tobias, D and Mendelsohn, R (1991) 'Valuing Ecotourism in a Tropical Rain-Forest Reserve' *Ambio*, vol 20, no 2, April, pp 91–93

Turner, K and Jones, T (1991) *Wetlands: Market and Intervention Failures – Four Case Studies* Earthscan, London

US Department of Agricultural (1990) Resources and Technology Division, Economic Research Service, *Climate Change: Economic Implications for World Agriculture* Washington DC, November (draft)

US Environmental Protection Agency (1985) *Costs and Benefits of Reducing Lead in Gasoline: Final Regulatory Impact Analysis* EPA-230-05-85-006, Washington DC, February

US Environmental Protection Agency (1987) *EPA's Use of Benefit-Cost Analysis 1981–1986* EPA-230-05-87-028, Washington DC, August

Walsh, R et al (1984) 'Valuing Option, Existence and Bequest Demands for Wilderness' *Land Economics*, vol 60, no 1

Whittington, D et al (1991) *Willingness to Pay for Improved Sanitation in Kumasi, Ghana* Report to the Infrastructure and Urban Development Department, World Bank, Washington DC, March

Willis, K and Benson, J (1988) 'Valuation of Wildlife: A Case Study on the Upper Teesdale Site of Special Scientific Interest and Comparison of Methods in Environmental Economics' in R K Turner (ed) *Sustainable Environmental Management* Belhaven Press, London

World Bank (1988) *Madagascar – Environmental Action Plan* July

World Bank (1990a) *Towards the Development of an Environmental Action Plan for Nigeria* World Bank, December

World Bank (1990b) *Hungary – Environmental Issues* Washington DC, November

World Bank (1990c) *Towards the Development of an Environmental Action Plan*

for Nigeria Western Africa Department, December
World Commission on Environment and Development (1987) *Our Common
Future* Oxford University Press, Oxford and New York

Further recommended reading

Barde, J-Ph and Pearce, D W (1991) *Valuing the Environment* Earthscan, London

Bentkover, J (ed) (1986) *Benefits Assessment: the State of the Art* Reidel, Dordrecht

Bojo, J, Maler, K-G and Unemo, L (1990) *Environment and Development: an Economic Approach* Kluwer, Dordrecht

Braden, J and Kolstad, C (1991) *Measuring the Demand for Environmental Quality* North Holland–Elsevier, Amsterdam

Carson, R and Mitchell, R (1989) *Using Surveys to Value Public Goods: the Contingent Valuation Method* Resources for the Future, Washington DC

Cummings, R et al (1986) *Valuing Environmental Goods: an Assessment of the Contingent Valuation Method* Rowman and Allenheld, Totowa

Freeman, A M (1979) *The Benefits of Environmental Improvement* Johns Hopkins University Press, Baltimore

Johansson, P-O (1987) *The Economic Theory and Measurement of Environmental Benefits* Cambridge University Press, Cambridge

Kneese, A (1984) *Measuring the Benefits of Clean Air and Water* Resources for the Future, Washington DC

Pearce, D W and Markandya, A (1989) *Environmental Policy Benefits: Monetary Valuation* OECD, Paris

Pearce, D W and Warford, J (1992) *World Without End: Environment, Economics and Sustainable Development* Oxford University Press, New York and Oxford

Turner, R K and Bateman, I (1990) *A Critical Review of Monetary Assessment Methods and Techniques* Environmental Appraisal Group, University of East Anglia, Norwich

Winpenny, J (1991) *Values for the Environment* HMSO, London

Index

afforestation
  investment in 63
  in Nigeria 38–9
African elephant 82–3
agriculture, effects of global
  warming on 24–5
air pollution
  OECD and 100–1
  in USA 34–5
avertive expenditures 112

basic needs 77
benefit-cost analysis
  and choice of technology 39–41
  and policy changes 44
  and polluter pays principle 41–4
  and programme appraisal 39
  and project appraisal 35–9
  of sectoral priorities 34–5
best available technology 5
biological diversity 82–9
birds, economic value of 83
Boulding, Kenneth 1–2
Brazil, rural water supply in 78
Burkina Faso, resource degradation
  in 27

capital stock 49–51, 57
carbon tax 43–4, 98, 99
carrying capacity 49
choice 1–5
command and control policies 42–3
contingent valuation 73–4, 78,
  106–7, 116
cowboy economy 1–2

debt-for-nature swaps 65–8

decision-making, and valuation
  14–15
desertification 81–2
developed countries
  discount rates in 59–60
  valuation exercises in 63
developing countries
  sustainable development in 62
  valuation in 11–12, 93–4
development 11–12, 34
  and environmental damage 29–30
  measures of 30–1
discount rate
  consumer discount rates 58–60
  estimation of 59
  modification of 55–60
  producer discount rates 60
  synthetic discount rates 60–1
  zero discount rates 57–8
discounting 6–9, 54–61
distributional weights 10
dose-response approach 27, 105,
  110–11
drugs 84–9
  value of 85–9
dung, valuation of 80–1

Earth Summit 62, 85
Eastern Europe 62–3
economic growth 95–104
economic rate of return 37–9
ecotourism 83–4
egalitarianism 8–9
endangered species 74–7
environmental damage
  and development 29–30
  national cost estimates of 23–9